The New Science Teacher: Cultivating Good Practice
Deborah Trumbull

Inventing Science Education for the New Millennium
Paul DeHart Hurd

Improving Teaching and Learning in Science and Mathematics
David F. Treagust, Reinders Duit, and Barry J. Fraser, Editors

Reforming Mathematics Education in America's Cities:
The Urban Mathematics Collaborative Project
Norman L. Webb and Thomas A. Romberg, Editors

What Children Bring to Light:
A Constructivist Perspective on Children's Learning in Science
Bonnie L. Shapiro

STS Education: International Perspectives on Reform
Joan Solomon and Glen Aikenhead, Editors

Reforming Science Education:
Social Perspectives and Personal Reflections
Rodger W. Bybee

THE NEW SCIENCE TEACHER

Cultivating Good Practice

DEBORAH J. TRUMBULL

FOREWORD BY D. JEAN CLANDININ

TEACHERS
COLLEGE
PRESS

Teachers College, Columbia University
New York and London

Much of the research in this book was supported through Hatch projects 137-444 and 137-411, USDA, 1987–1994.

Published by Teachers College Press, 1234 Amsterdam Avenue, New York, NY 10027

Library of Congress Cataloging-in-Publication Data

Trumbull, Deborah J.
    The new science teacher : cultivating good practice / Deborah J.
Trumbull ; foreword by D. Jean Clandinin.
        p.   cm. — (Ways of knowing in science series)
    Includes bibliographical references and index.
    ISBN 0-8077-3875-1 (cloth). — ISBN 0-8077-3874-3 (pbk.)
    1. Biology—Study and teaching.   2. Biology teachers Interviews.
I. Title.   II. Series.
    QH315.T77   1999
    570'.71—dc21   99-33355

ISBN 0-8077-3874-3 (paper)
ISBN 0-8077-3875-1 (cloth)

Printed on acid-free paper
Manufactured in the United States of America

06   05   04   03   02   01   00   99   8   7   6   5   4   3   2   1

In memory of Jack Easley,
who helped me learn to listen more deeply.

Contents

Foreword

As I read Deborah Trumbull's manuscript and thought about writing this foreword for her book, I was fortunate to have Annie Davies, a former doctoral student and teacher researcher, as a house guest. Annie and I have worked together on many projects over the years. Together, we planned and lived out an alternative collaborative program in teacher education and, with Pat Hogan and Barbara Kennard, wrote a book about the program and teacher education. We share various research projects in the area of teacher knowledge, particularly projects where we try to understand how school contexts, what we call professional knowledge landscapes, shape and are shaped by teachers. We spend hours talking about our work as teachers, hers as a teacher of children and mine as a university teacher of adults. Deborah's manuscript made an intriguing piece that fit with our shared interests, and we spent the weekend reading and talking about what it called us to consider.

It called up many topics for those of us who tell stories of ourselves as teachers, as teacher educators, and as researchers. In this foreword I share some of the topics of the conversations Annie and I had, as a way of suggesting who I think are possible readers of the book. Deborah's book is about students becoming teachers and about listening to their stories of how they have changed. It is a longitudinal study, so we stay with these teachers for a long time, following them from their Cornell teacher education program into their first few years of teaching. There are six teachers, seven when you count Deborah, and she tells enough of her story that we get a sense that we can learn from her story, too.

Annie and I have worked with student teachers, she from the place of a cooperating teacher and I from my university place. We liked what Deborah believes about teachers, that is, that teachers should reflect on their practices and that teachers should think of teaching as a research activity. Annie and I share these beliefs and try to live them out in our own teaching and in our work with teachers learning to teach. We share Deborah's belief in constant reflection and rethinking on practice, whether one is a student or a teacher educator.

But Annie and I know what a struggle it is to maintain this story of teacher education on a university landscape where the institutional narrative calls for competition and exams and grades. It is hard to keep the focus on reflection and community when the institutional script keeps refocusing the student teachers' eyes elsewhere. What becomes apparent in Deborah's research is that this is a conflicting story for her and the student teachers, although there is additional complexity because the student teachers arrive with an embodied knowing of this story line of competition for grades. In Deborah's research the instructional narrative, as well as the embodied narrative knowing of the students, conflicts with the reflective practice stories of the teacher education program.

The context, the landscape, continues to shape the beginning teachers when they move to working in schools. This work resonated for Annie and me as we made links among our own stories, the stories of student teachers with whom we have worked, and the stories of teachers with whom we live in community. It was refreshing, albeit discomforting, to read stories of the teachers who worked with Deborah and to see similar themes being lived out in their stories. They quickly learned to live what we call in our work "cover stories" as they played the game required of them in schools. Annie and I began to talk at length about what teacher education can, should, or might do to respond to the shaping influences of school contexts. We wondered how those of us who work in teacher education, either at the university or in schools, could respond to the concerns about the shaping influences of context. As we read and talked about the stories of Sylvie, Maggie, and the others, we wondered how their experiences could be read back into teacher education programs in order to find other possibilities for re-imagining teacher education that would be a competing story with the story now in place.

We were interested to read the careful case studies of the teachers to see how the placement of the teachers in particular schools shaped how they came to know themselves as teachers. The teachers were shaped into the "kind of teacher" that the particular school wanted. We wondered about how those of us in teacher education could address this troubling issue. Deborah shares our wonder about how to support students as reflective practitioners in schools. Reading the accounts, constructed over years, we see the subtle ways that teachers are shaped by their school landscapes. We wondered how we could, in conversation and with imagination, find ways to shape school landscapes that would engender support for reflective practice?

The work with student teachers, writes Deborah, has changed her understanding of what it means to be a teacher educator. These comments reminded Annie and me that we, too, found that our work with student teachers influenced us profoundly. In our final chapter of *Learning to Teach: Teaching to Learn* (1993), we wrote that we are all learning to teach whether we are positioned as cooperating teachers, student teachers, or university teachers. Deborah drew our attention to similar thoughts.

We had a long talk about inquiry teaching, a topic that appears and reappears in the accounts of the student teachers. They are science teachers trying to engage their students in science. Neither Annie nor I have taught high school science, but Annie has worked with science teaching with grade-3 children. She spoke of a unit she taught not so long ago on meal worms, a unit in which she encouraged the grade-3 children to ask their own questions about meal worms and then to explore ways to inquire into their questions. Their questions were many, and they designed experiments to find answers to these questions. As we talked about the teachers in Deborah's study, we noticed they spoke often about the concept of open-ended labs and whether they were doing what they were supposed to do. As Elaine, one of the teachers, said, "The labs I did weren't great." Again we wondered about whether there is a place to use these conversations and dilemmas to inform our teacher education practices. How can we engage our programs and ourselves with these questions?

As we came to the end of our weekend together and the richness of our talk, Annie and I realized that new research agendas, new research puzzles, were opened for us. We worked our way through the manuscript, stopping along the way, asking each other questions, calling up stories from our experiences, and beginning to set our stories alongside the accounts Deborah included. As we did this, we realized this is a powerful way to read this book. It needs to be read not as a set of prescriptions or problems to be solved, but as an invitation to wonder. The gaps and silences that are part of the accounts of the six teachers provide spaces for us to wonder, for us to ask questions about how we can engage ourselves and our students in more reflective practice.

D. Jean Clandinin
Centre for Research for Teacher
Education and Development
University of Alberta

Preface

Prospective biology teachers begin university teacher education programs with conceptualizations of teaching biology that have developed through their own experiences as successful students, gained in many classrooms over many years. They frequently enter teacher education programs that challenge their ideas by presenting alternative views of teaching and learning, based on some vision of reform. Once they complete teacher education programs, new teachers enter schools where practices engender particular conceptualizations of biology teaching. The conceptualizations of biology teaching that are promulgated in these different settings are not all consistent. A lack of consistency across contexts can impose stresses on new teachers and render their professional development complex. What views prevail as people develop as teachers? How do they manage the contradictions across the different conceptualizations? How do they succeed in their contexts of practice as new teachers?

In this book I report on a longitudinal study to examine the ideas that six new teachers had about teaching biology, in order to see how these ideas were shaped by the teachers' experiences and how their ideas shaped their interpretations of their experiences. Interviews with the new teachers began when they were enrolled in a teacher education program and continued through their first 2 or 3 years of practice. The teacher education program these students completed was designed to prepare teachers who would be innovative, concerned with helping all their students understand biology deeply and fully, and committed to continuing professional development and improvement.

This book documents the struggles of the six new teachers to develop their own visions for themselves as teachers and to survive and thrive in their diverse settings. The book is based on interviews and observations over a 5- or 6-year period and focuses on three areas important to biology teaching. These areas, as I will show, are interrelated in a number of ways. First, I looked at the new teachers' conceptualizations of learning, examining such issues as how they know when they or others understand, what things are necessary to support learning, and what conditions they feel hinder learning.

Second, I analyzed the new teachers' views about the discipline of biology and about the purposes for teaching biology in secondary school. Many of the current reform proposals for teacher education focus on the importance of deep knowledge of subject matter. These six new teachers were all biology majors at a research university and thus should be assumed to have had excellent exposure to the field of biology.

Third, current reforms emphasize that learners should understand the nature of scientific inquiry. Laboratory teaching is cited frequently as the vehicle through which pupils can learn about the processes of scientific investigation. The book looks at the new teachers' ideas about laboratory teaching in biology and their experiences in laboratories.

The book portrays the ideas of new teachers and examines what happens when they assume their first teaching positions. It looks at what conditions support their development as innovative teachers and what conditions make it more difficult for them. In this time of increased emphasis on reform in science teaching, what impact does this national emphasis have on new teachers in their schools?

By focusing on these three areas, I also explicate some of the concerns that face science teacher educators. For example, if new biology teachers are to have a solid grasp of their discipline, what should science teacher educators know? How much biology should they know and how should they use this knowledge in teaching education courses? How do teacher educators work with students who are unsure of themselves as biology learners and what kinds of support are needed?

And, possibly the most important role of this book, what is it like to be a new teacher? What are the pressures that new teachers face? In a profession where isolation and individualism seem to be the rule, these stories can help new teachers, and all of us who work with new teachers, to understand their lives and, it is to be hoped, to respond more productively to their needs.

MY POSITION AS RESEARCHER

I became a science teacher educator serendipitously. After earning a master's degree in biology, I taught first-year science classes and/or human anatomy and physiology at three different community colleges for 10 years. These years were interrupted by three semesters of doctoral study in neurobiology and behavior at Cornell University that ended when my husband-to-be moved to Canada. I had become involved in extensive curriculum and staff development work at my last community college, an experience that convinced me I should earn a doctorate in education. I entered a program at the University of Illinois in Champaign–Urbana, convinced that I knew all there was about education and needed only a credential. My arrogance and ignorance quickly were replaced by fascination with the complexities and uncertainties of the field. At Illinois I worked on evaluation projects with Robert Stake and Jack Easley and did a dissertation that looked at teachers' perspectives. However, I considered myself not a teacher educator but an educational psychologist with a specialization in program evaluation and qualitative research.

These were the areas in which I taught at my first university position, although the writing I worked on examined teachers' knowledge and my own evolving conceptions of biology teaching (Trumbull, 1987, 1990). My first job was not a good one, and when a position at Cornell was advertised in 1986, I applied and was accepted. The Cornell position enabled me to integrate the disparate experiences of my past.

My colleagues and I at Cornell had the chance to design a new program for the preparation of secondary science and mathematics teachers. We planned to design a program to prepare teachers who would be committed to helping their pupils develop deep understandings of content and a faith in their abilities to learn. We planned for a year, influenced by the existing research at Cornell that included work on conceptual change theory (Posner, Strike, Hewson, & Gertzog, 1982; and later, Strike & Posner, 1992) and D. B. Gowin and J. D. Novak's work on meaningful learning (Novak & Gowin, 1984). I will describe these approaches in some detail later. The important point to mention here is that we believed that these theories implied a view of science teaching and learning that contrasted with many of our students' prior experiences and their own beliefs. A colleague hired after me, William Carlsen, came up with the name and acronym for our new program—Teacher Education in Science and Mathematics (TESM).

I conducted my study because I believed it was crucial for teachers to reflect on their own practice. If I were trying to educate reflective practitioners, I felt it imperative that I reflect on my own teaching and on my assumptions and beliefs (Grimmett & Erickson, 1988; McNiff, 1993; Schön, 1983). To study my work, I chose to learn about the ideas that my students held when they began TESM and to follow how these changed. I did not plan an evaluation study in which I would determine how much their ideas moved to match those of the TESM program or how well TESM worked to change their ideas. Rather, I wanted to understand their ideas more fully than I could as their teacher and in the process to explicate and refine my own conceptions and commitments. I call the people in my study new teachers, because as soon as they entered the TESM program they began to think of themselves as teachers. I chose to focus on biology teachers because of my long experience teaching biology.

My study quickly became more complex than I had envisioned. I started with a simple plan—I, or a research assistant, would ask them questions about their experiences and from their answers infer their views of learning, teaching, biology, and laboratory work. I would then trace the evolution of these ideas over time and look for factors that shaped that evolution. However, it soon became clear that these ideas were part of a larger conceptual ecology (Strike & Posner, 1992) that included not only a host of interrelated ideas but also values, emotions, and personal development. To do justice to these new teachers, my analyses became more holistic and took far longer than I originally anticipated.

I was directly involved in the lives of the six new teachers. I taught the first course all TESM students took. When Pat and Fred were students, George Posner, Bill Carlsen, and I taught that course together, but for the 2 years after that I taught the course alone. I served on the graduate committees of all six new teachers, supervised three in student teaching, and taught the pre-student teaching seminar for four. The TESM program had no more than 14 students in a cohort during my study. I was well-acquainted with the new teachers, and they had many opportunities to experience my teaching. There were also numerous opportunities for informal interactions at program and departmental events. My relations with the new teachers certainly would have shaped their conversations with me, but I was careful to interview students when I no longer had responsibility for giving them grades. Of course, any researcher elicits a reaction from the people she works to know. I hope that they perceived me as someone who cared for them, who was sincerely interested in learning about their concerns and in using what I learned to improve my own practice. In my interviews with the new teachers and in informal conversations during my visits to them, I was generally careful not to offer explicit suggestions unless asked. There were times when I pointed out things they did that I thought were good and times when they asked me my opinion about things that they did. I did not want my conversations to have any flavor of evaluation. At times I may have carried this attempt at neutrality too far and prevented myself from asking probing questions.

THE ORGANIZATION OF THE BOOK

Chapter 1 describes the context of my study. It begins with a description of the six new teachers in their third year after completing the teacher education program. The next section summarizes views of teaching and learning relevant to my study. This is followed by sections on reforms in science education, the role of laboratory teaching in science, conceptual change teaching and teacher education, and the TESM program. Chapter 1 concludes with a description of the methods used and a discussion of how the study evolved. Chapters 2 through 7 present the stories of the six new teachers. The chapters that present the new teachers begin with biographical information about the person. I illustrate the evolution of their views, using extensive verbatim quotes from our interviews during their preservice years. Then I rely on observations and interview remarks to illustrate their teaching practice. Each case study ends with a summary that provides an overview of the new teachers' changes in thinking and practice. Chapter 8 returns to the initial questions.

CONVENTIONS USED IN THE STORIES

When I quote the new teachers, I modify their spoken language to remove repetition, such as sentence fragments that begin a thought that then is expressed more fully in the next sentence. I remove qualifiers when they are used habitually by the new teachers, terms such as "kind of" or "sort of." I also remove any catch phrases that the new teachers rely on, phrases such as "you know," or "it's like." Indicating larger chunks of omitted material required judgment, since the standard conventions were designed to indicate changes in printed texts. As anyone who has transcribed speech knows, we often do not talk in sentences, so as the transcriber I imposed sentences to make the transcripts readable. I use three ellipses in the middle of a sentence to indicate omitted phrases. I use four ellipses to show that I have omitted larger blocks of transcript, at least one full sentence. I use dashes to indicate the interviewee's pauses for thinking. When I add words to make the meaning more clear, I put the words in brackets. I put information about nonverbal sounds in parentheses. I have used extensive quotes for four reasons: (1) to represent the new teachers' views fully, (2) to provide some glimpse into their ways of thinking, or at least of expressing their thinking, (3) to provide evidence to support my interpretations of their ideas, (4) to give readers the chance to interpret for themselves.

CHAPTER 1

Contexts of the Study

In the third year after completing the TESM program, two of the new teachers were no longer in the classroom. George was working on a research degree in biology and did not expect to return to secondary teaching, although he realized that he would be teaching in some capacity in his career as a research biologist. Maggie was working at a Teacher Center, organizing science in-service programs for experienced teachers. She reported being a bit surprised that some of the teachers with whom she worked were not especially reflective.

Sylvie, after switching from an urban high school in midyear, was teaching middle school general science in a small rural high school. She had her own classroom, adorned with many artifacts and animals left by the former teacher. She appeared comfortable in this school and had forged a vision of what she hoped to accomplish in her teaching. She relied on the school curriculum for planning and welcomed that support. Elaine was teaching biology in a suburban high school for the third year and finally had her own classroom, which was decorated with commercial posters, materials produced by students for various projects, and shelves holding equipment. Elaine was teaching both college-preparatory and non-college-preparatory students, and was excited about helping the lower-track students gain confidence in learning biology. She had designed a number of her own exercises to use with students and had developed a reputation in the school, whereby students came to expect certain activities and projects they had heard she used the year before. Fred was teaching secondary biology in a small rural school, in the room he had used for 3 years. Slowly he had emptied the room of the materials accumulated over several years and by previous teachers. He was teaching both college-preparatory and non-college-prep classes, and had developed procedures for administering mastery learning in his classes. He was fully fluent in the mandated state curriculum and had no doubt that his students would do well on the end-of-the-year test, a success important to his tenure. Pat was teaching physical science in a small-town junior high school, after having taught life sciences the year before. Her class-

1

room was decorated with commercial posters and materials made by her students. Even though she was a biologist, she loved teaching physical science because there were so many hands-on materials she could use with her students. She hoped to make them aware that scientific explanations of many common phenomena exist, although she was not concerned that they remember the explanations completely. Because she taught seventh grade the year before, she was working with most of her students for a second year, which she enjoyed.

VIEWS OF TEACHING AND LEARNING SALIENT TO MY WORK

Meaningful Learning

The research in science education that I read views learning as an active process that requires learners to grapple with the content until they develop their own understandings that will be long-lasting and useful. Novak and Gowin (1984) used a term, *meaningful learning*, first used by David Ausubel, to describe this kind of learning, and investigated strategies that would facilitate meaningful learning. In contrast to meaningful learning, rote learning is the kind of learning too often encouraged in schools. Although rote learning can enable students to pass tests successfully, it is ephemeral and not integrated with the learners' existing knowledge.

Students' Alternative Frameworks

A number of researchers in the 1980s looked carefully at students' thinking about many science topics and found that students held ideas alternative to the ones taught in science classes. These students' alternative ideas persisted despite exposure to accepted orthodox explanations taught to them (e.g., Driver, Guesne, & Tiberghien, 1985; Gilbert, Osborne, & Fensham, 1982; Gunstone, White, & Fensham, 1988; Helm & Novak, 1983; West & Pines, 1985). Science educators were concerned about these alternative ideas not merely because they wanted their pupils to have the most current knowledge but also because these alternative ideas could lead individuals to make bad choices in their lives. Documentation of students' alternative frameworks caused science educators to realize that learning required more than the acquisition of new information. As an experienced teacher I found research on students' alternative ideas appealing because it made sense of many of my observations. I had found that there were some student ideas that persisted despite my elaborate efforts. Knowing that these were not simply wrong answers or mistakes, or symptoms of my failure, was helpful, but I was then compelled to seek reasons for the persistence of these alternative frameworks. I had to think about just how the person had constructed the alternative ideas and why they remained useful.

Conceptual Change Theory

Posner, Strike, Hewson, and Gertzog (1982) provided a model of learning that illuminated the complexity of the changes involved. They used Kuhn's notion of paradigm and paradigm shift (Kuhn, 1970) as a metaphor for the change that resulted when a learner developed a deep understanding in science. Deep understanding required a fundamental shift in the way the learner viewed the world and the development of a new conceptualization that greatly altered pre-existing ideas. Posner and colleagues and Strike and Posner (1992) argued that it was not enough for teachers to merely present learners with facts and concepts from the orthodox framework or theory. Teachers first had to grasp how learners conceptualized the idea or phenomenon, then present the orthodox view in a way that was intelligible to the learners, and then demonstrate that this was a plausible framework. Further, the learners had to realize that the orthodox framework was more fruitful, that it could explain and relate more topics and produce further thought. A conceptual change view of learning is closely related to the view called constructivism.

Constructivism

Rosalind Driver (Driver, Asoko, Leach, Mortimer, & Scott, 1994) was one of the researchers who devoted extensive effort to explicating constructivism and documenting pedagogical approaches that would engender conceptual change. Constructivism is a term used rather loosely of late, but a number of notions are central to its more rigorous form. Learning is an active process that requires the learner to engage fully with thinking about and using the content in a range of situations. Many constructivist scholars such as Driver consider that dialogue, argument, and reference to evidence are essential to developing new frameworks and understandings. (See also Cobb, 1994, for an overview.) One aspect that I consider central to a rigorous view of constructivism is that there is no one technique espoused for ensuring learning. Constructivism provides a way to look at teaching and learning activities but does not dictate any specific teaching techniques. These must be developed by teachers to suit their situations. In a sense, constructivism can seem unhelpful because it does not come with a set of methods or techniques that can be learned and then applied. It is, however, a view that can guide the reflection of teachers because it provides a framework through which to analyze learning and teaching.

REFORMS IN SCIENCE EDUCATION

As I conducted my research, large prestigious national organizations in the United States were attempting to lead efforts to reform science teaching. Many of the concerns addressed in reform documents from the 1990s echoed concerns of earlier reform efforts, although there were some differences. One of the significant prior reform efforts in biology teaching was headed by J. J. Schwab. Schwab helped to establish the Biological Sciences Curriculum Studies project (BSCS) in 1958 to provide leadership and direction to secondary biology teachers. Unlike other projects of that period, the BSCS is still active. A brief history of the biology curriculum supplied in one of the BSCS documents (BSCS, 1970) presents some of the tensions in the teaching of biology and is worth presenting here. In the period from 1890 to 1921, "the biology curriculum and its texts were almost entirely descriptive. They consisted almost wholly of a mass of disconnected facts and elementary generalizations" (BSCS, 1970, p. 5). One point in favor of the curriculum was that it was determined by individuals who represented the current state of knowledge in biology, those working as scientists or closely associated with scientists. From 1929 to 1957, the biology curriculum was modified to meet the needs of an increasingly diverse student body and/or to conform to current educational theories about how youngsters learn. The result was that the biology curriculum no longer represented the most current knowledge in the field, nor did it represent the structure of the discipline. The BSCS began, in 1958, with the attempt to

> present a valid image of current biological science. A field of knowledge can be viewed in terms of major dimensions that aid in describing what constitutes the field. Three of these dimensions are the subjects to be investigated, the major generalizations and conceptual schemes which result from and give focus to investigation, and the modes of investigation. (BSCS, 1970, p. 9)

The 1970 *Teachers' Handbook* identified seven *levels* of organization at which biology can be investigated, from the level of the molecular to the level of the world biome. The *Handbook* stated nine *themes* central to biology. These were: change of living things over time; evolution; diversity of type and unity of pattern in living things; the genetic continuity of life; the complementarity of structure and function; regulation and homeostasis; preservation of life in the face of change; science as inquiry; and the history of biological conceptions.

DeBoer (1991) noted that over the years biology reform efforts have placed different emphases on three major areas: biology as a structured body of knowledge to be learned as a logically organized body; science as a set of investigative processes; and science as a human activity, including the application of technologies and its relation to the rest of society.

Current reform documents abound in the United States (e.g., American Association for the Advancement of Science, 1993; National Science Teachers Association, 1992). The *National Science Education Standards* (the *Standards*) appear to include all three emphases identified by DeBoer. The *Standards* include statements about biology teaching similar to the levels and themes from BSCS and include its emphasis on inquiry. They also place increased emphasis on "science in personal and social perspective," with the goal that students be able to "undertake sophisticated study of personal and societal challenges" (National Research Council, 1996, p. 167), including such things as the effects of technology on natural systems, the cycling of materials through the ecosystem, and choosing healthy diets. The *Standards* add "the history and nature of science," which looks at how people do science and how science knowledge has changed over time. The *Standards* also contain directives about the assessment of student learning. These assessment standards aim to increase the range of evidence used to evaluate student achievement to ensure that students "apply scientific knowledge and reasoning to situations similar to those they will encounter in the world outside their classroom as well as to situations that approximate how scientists do their work" (NRC, 1996, p. 78).

The content and purposes for biology teaching continue to be areas of debate that represent some of the issues and dilemmas inherent in schooling. One implication of a constructivist view of science learning is that the curriculum must contain less material in order to ensure that students have the time needed to develop deeper understandings. The temptation in introductory biology curricula is to include something about everything, generating a plethora of content and less emphasis on organizing themes or principles. The concern for a delimited curriculum is especially salient to biology teaching because the discipline is so complex.

Although the BSCS and the *Standards* identify different levels in the study of biology, they do not attend to the relationships between the fields studying these different levels, nor to the complexity that these levels add to thinking about the discipline as a unified field of study. Cummins and Remsen (1992) reviewed the work of Mayr (1982, 1988) and others and noted that "the many organizational levels (e.g. cell, tissue, organism, population, etc.) result in emergent properties at each higher level, explanations for which require examination of different levels of causation." In other words, knowing molecular biology does not enable one to predict how cells will behave, because there are other factors governing the behavior of cells.

Second, because of the multilevel nature of biology, the methods and assumptions used to study at one level may not be valid at other levels (Cummins & Remsen, 1992). Cummins (1995) also indicated that in many descriptions of science it often is assumed that experimental methods are the only ones used in biological investigations, an assumption that ignores the important role observational studies have played and continue to play in many fields of biology, including ecology, natural history, and evolutionary studies. Thus, biology teaching presents some challenges not recognized in many reform documents.

THE ROLE OF LABORATORY TEACHING

Laboratory work in biology generally has been considered the route through which to introduce learners to the procedures of scientific inquiry. However, the purposes of laboratory instruction have been the subject of debate for some time. An issue of the *International Journal of Science Education* examined the role of laboratory teaching in science. Hodson (1996) pointed out that, historically, laboratory teaching has been used to serve several, sometimes conflicting, purposes, including:

> motivating students by stimulating interest and enjoyment; teaching laboratory skills; assisting concept acquisition and development; developing an understanding of scientific inquiry and developing expertise in conducting inquiries; inculcating the so-called scientific attitudes; encouraging social skill development. (p. 756)

Hodson's response to these many goals was to argue for a narrowed focus for laboratory instruction. White (1996), in the same issue, was more concerned that teachers clarify the purposes for each specific laboratory activity to ensure it was serving that purpose. White implied that laboratory work legitimately could be used to meet a number of goals, but we must be clear about those goals. White (1996) also pointed out, regarding the learning of inquiry, that "the methods of science are much more complex than simple control of variables. As Woolnough (1991) points out, scientists do different things, and do not agree among themselves that there is *a* method"

(p. 764, emphasis in original). White referred to other authors who have noted that scientific investigations of all sorts contain a significant proportion of art and craft and that all science observations are shaped by theory, making an emphasis on teaching inquiry a more complex endeavor.

CONCEPTUAL CHANGE TEACHING AND TEACHER EDUCATION

Just as science learners come to science classes with conceptualizations of the phenomena to be studied, preservice teachers enter teacher education with existing conceptualizations based on many years of success in schools. A conceptual change perspective provides a fruitful way to think of teacher education efforts that hope to provide new teachers a new framework with which to think about teaching and learning (Stoddart, 1991; Stofflett, 1994; Stofflett & Stoddart, 1994). "Many preservice teacher education students carry with them views of teaching which, like many in the community, revolve around the belief that teaching content is a matter of telling or showing, also that learning means remembering" (McDiarmid, 1990, cited in Loughran, 1994, p. 366). The TESM program certainly hoped that its teachers would think and teach differently than they had been taught.

THE TESM PROGRAM

When we planned the TESM program, we assumed that our teachers had to have a solid grasp of their discipline, so we required them all to complete a full major, take foundational education classes, and do early field work in schools. These decisions necessitated a fifth year of study. We did not plan any traditional methods classes but instead developed a two-semester course sequence. The first TESM course, which became my course, was called Knowing and Learning in Science and Mathematics. (I have described this course in more detail in Trumbull, 1991; Trumbull & Slack, 1991.) Students had to design, conduct, and analyze interviews with non-science students to learn how they thought about some concrete instance that instantiated a key science notion. For example, one of the new teachers interviewed other Cornell students about the last time they had a cold. The conversation that resulted—and even young college students love to talk about their symptoms—enabled Elaine to analyze their conceptualizations of disease, including the causal agents for colds, the immune reaction, spread of disease, and treatment processes. In requiring these interview projects, it was our belief that future teachers would realize that even other Cornell students held stable and sensible explanations that did not correspond to the orthodox explanations they must have studied in high school or college. Further, we hoped that analyzing these interviews would cause the new teachers to reflect on their own understandings of their disciplines and realize areas that they needed to study further to gain a deeper understanding. While they were enrolled in this class, the new teachers served as tutors for introductory biology courses on campus.

The second TESM course, Observing Instruction in Science and Mathematics, required that the new teachers spend several hours each week observing in secondary classes. The course provided three frameworks or lenses through which students were to observe. Students focused successively on curriculum, classroom interactions and discourse patterns, and instructional approaches.

Student teaching was completed during the fall semester of the fifth year. It was preceded by an intensive full-day seminar that lasted on average 3 weeks. This seminar involved microteaching exercises and lecture/discussion on topics such as classroom management and discipline, lesson planning, and test and homework development. All the faculty involved in TESM supervised student teaching, making six visits during the course of the semester-long practicum. We developed an assignment we called the On-going Assignment (OGA) that accompanied student teaching. Some of the OGA was to be written prior to the start of the actual teaching, in which the new teachers had to describe the school community. After reviewing the curriculum they would be teaching, they had to select one unit and develop a unit plan. The unit plan had to justify the importance of the content and its inclusion in one unit and relate it to the rest of the course material. New teachers then had to describe methods they would use to engage students with the material and ways they would use to evaluate student understanding. During their actual teaching, the new teachers had to describe how and why they had modified their plans, what they had learned about their pupils through working with them. We also asked the new teachers to describe how they felt they were fitting into the school system. The new teachers wrote drafts of OGA sections throughout their actual student teaching. The final section, completed after student teaching, consisted of an analysis of their work and reflection on their teaching. Students rewrote their initial drafts and defended the OGA at the end of the student teaching semester. In the spring semester after student teaching, the new teachers took courses in their disciplines or in cognate areas.

While the six new teachers were in TESM, there was generous funding from the Andrew W. Mellon Foundation and an anonymous donor. This funding supported work with youngsters with backgrounds different from that of the new teachers for one summer and a second summer of study at Shoals Marine Laboratory in a course called Adaptations of Marine Organisms.

METHODS OF THE STUDY AND EVOLUTION OF THE RESEARCH

Data Gathering

I worked with two new teachers from each of three successive cohorts in the TESM program. The interviews took place over an 8-year period as I followed them through the third year of teaching. Figure 1.1 charts when these teachers were interviewed and observed.

All of the new teachers whom I interviewed volunteered for the study during their junior year. I was concerned that students not feel any pressure to volunteer, so I announced the study, passed out consent forms, and waited. All the students whom I followed for the full study were European-Americans. Looking back on my records I realize I did not follow up on some initial interviews I had done with students from other backgrounds. I am appalled by this now because I am afraid that it reveals the freedom that those of us of European-American backgrounds have to ignore diversity because it has not been of direct concern for us.

I did consciously select for uniformity of background by choosing to interview students who majored in biology. I had much tacit knowledge about biology teaching, which I trusted would enable me to ask better questions and make better sense of responses.

When the new teachers were enrolled in the TESM program, interviews focused on their interpretations of their experiences as students at Cornell,

FIGURE 1.1 Chronology of Interviews and Observations of the New Teachers

Year 1	2	3	4	5	6	7	8
Fred *junior*	Fred *senior*	Fred *MAT*		Fred 2	Fred 3		
Pat *junior*	Pat *senior*	Pat *MAT*		Pat 2	Pat 3		
		Elaine *senior*	Elaine *MAT*		Elaine 1	Elaine 2	Elaine 3
		Sylvie *senior*	Sylvie *MAT*		Sylvie 1	Sylvie 2	Sylvie 3
		George *junior*		George *MAT*	George 1	George 2	
		Maggie *junior*	Maggie *senior*	Maggie *MAT*	Maggie 1	Maggie 2	

The new teachers' names are followed by the year in the program or a number representing the year of teaching.

in classes and in their field work, and addressed how they became interested in studying science, what they thought distinguished science from other disciplines, how they would describe themselves as learners, what they thought important about laboratory work, what the purposes for teaching introductory biology are, what kinds of students they had helped, and how they could tell whether others understand something. The interviews were loosely structured. We made every attempt to follow the interviewees' ideas as they emerged in the interview conversation. (See Mishler, 1986, for more discussion.) I transcribed nearly all the interviews myself. For the ones I did not transcribe, I listened to the tapes with the transcripts and made any needed corrections. I did verbatim transcriptions, including all interviewer interjections. I sent copies of the transcripts to each teacher throughout the study, with instructions to correct or amplify as they wished.

Once they were employed, I visited the new teachers at their schools and spent a full day with each of them, which provided many chances for observations and casual conversations. When our schedules allowed, I took them out to dinner before or after spending the day. During my visits, I talked with their principals or assistant principals, and often chatted with other teachers, perhaps in the lunchroom or at an informal event. When the new teachers were doing laboratory activities, I assisted their students. The formal interviews were conducted during the teachers' free times, sometimes during the school day, sometimes after school, and usually both.

I began the interviews by asking about things I had observed. At some point in these interviews I would ask the new teachers to compare and contrast pairs of students. I initially had thought about using a version of the Kelly Repertory Grid (Kelly, 1955) to analyze responses, but found the technique too constraining. However, discussions about students were very productive because they surfaced detail about the new teacher's practice and purposes and ideas.

Data Analysis

When I started the project, I read through transcripts, making notes, marking important instances, and using them to guide the next interviews with that teacher. Near the middle of the study I purchased a software program that allowed me to move marked segments into secondary files. For example, I could code all remarks in all the interviews that referred to biology and move these to a separate file. Once I accumulated this file, I could more easily compare the conceptions expressed by the new teachers and note similarities and contrasts. The program also allowed me to trace a segment back to the original interview, to recontextualize remarks when needed. Once I had categorized remarks and identified key quotes that represented the views of the teachers, I prepared long case studies of each teacher, using these extensive quotes. I sent these case studies, generally 60 pages long, to each new teacher, asking for their reactions and comments. They all returned the case studies or told me they were fine. For this book, I reduced the long case studies by focusing on three areas: learning, the nature of biology and purposes for teaching biology, and the role of laboratory instruction in biology teaching.

After I decided not to use the repertory grid technique to analyze the interviews, I attempted to do a sequential analysis, in which the categories I determined the first year for Pat and Fred would guide the analyses of the interviews with the next pair, be revised, and guide the analyses of the next pair. This orderly sequential process did not work, for two reasons. My continued experiences changed what I regarded as salient, and each new teacher's experiences led me to re-examine earlier interviews. It was only by working with all of the interviews of all of the teachers that I could develop an interpretation with which I was comfortable. (Brown & Gilligan 1992, evocatively explore some of the challenges of analyzing longitudinal data.)

The Research Approach

Not only did my data analyses change over time, but my understanding of what I was doing changed. When I started my study, process–product research was waning. Process–product research attempted to find correlations between observed teacher behaviors and student learning. Once correlations were found, new teachers could be trained in those behaviors, with the expectation that their students, too, would show improved learning (for a review see Clark & Peterson, 1986). Process–product research made precise observation of teacher behaviors and student learning imperative. I felt that such precision distorted the work of teachers. I began my study strongly influenced by a line of research that sought to explicate teachers' beliefs and thinking about their work (e.g., Calderhead, 1987; Nespor, 1987). The expectation of this research was that understanding teachers' ideas would furnish better understandings of the reasons for their actions. I felt that the emphasis on teachers' thinking fit well with conceptual change theory as I understood it, so I set out to design an interview guide that would elicit the new teachers' thinking. I did not plan to gather systematic data about the teachers' behaviors or about their students' learning because these areas were outside the intent of my study.

I was also very much influenced by work in qualitative research and wanted to do an interpretive study that would be flexible and enable me to modify procedures as necessary to follow up on the things that emerged as important. Interpretivism assumes that any understanding of the events of another's life requires examination of the individual, the context in which he or she lives, and his or her interpretations of that context. Another central tenet is that there is no one definitive interpretation, although there are better and worse interpretations (e.g., Erickson, 1986; Taylor, 1982). The interpreter makes her case as cogently and coherently as possible, using and citing relevant evidence in enough detail to allow the reader to question the interpretation (Louden, 1995). For example, in responding to a review of his 1991 book, Louden (1995) wrote, "I deliberately wrote the book in a way that lends itself to a variety of readings. . . . [The reviewer] cannot, however, exhaust the meaning of the text in one interpretation" (p. 112). Good interpretations, however well-argued, are still tenuous and partial. This sentence is quite easy to write, but very difficult to live. During the course of this study I had to grapple with my fear that I just was not getting it right, even though I said I believed that there was no one right interpretation. My belief in multiple possible interpretations led me to present stories of the new teachers rather than develop some overarching model.

Continued work on teacher thinking also made my findings more tenuous. Nespor and Barylske (1991) pointed out that in research interviews, when teachers talk about themselves to researchers, they are "not revealing but crafting and constructing, those 'selves'" (p. 811). So, too, when I interacted with the new teachers as their professor or observed them at work, we were each creating selves within the particular setting, framed by our roles, our histories together and separately.

The final factor that sent me into fits of anxiety is something obvious after reading textbooks on qualitative research approaches. Data gathering and analysis are not processes fully driven by explicit techniques, but depend on insight. My relation to these new teachers has been complex and has developed over an extended time. I have used knowledge from a host of interactions in framing and analyzing my conversations with the new teachers. As Gudmundsdottir (1996) pointed out, much of our sense making is informal and not explicit. The degree to which any researcher can make these tacit processes explicit is a matter of debate (see, for example, Peshkin, 1985, 1988; Buchmann, 1992). My perspective is shaped by my care for these six people, for whom I wish the best and in whose lives I have played some role. A large part of my analysis consisted of working to develop an empathic understanding of the lives of these new teachers, to imagine what it must have been like to be them, going through these experiences, and then to portray that understanding.

Max Van Manen's conception of a hermeneutic phenomenology clarified many of my nascent ideas about research because I was myself changed.

From a phenomenological point of view, to do research is always to question the way we experience the world, to want to know the world in which we live as human beings. And since to *know* the world is profoundly to *be* in the world in a certain way, the act of researching-questioning-theorizing is the intentional act of attaching ourselves to the world, to become more fully part of it, or better, to *become* the world. (Van Manen, 1990, p. 5, emphasis in original)

Why Stories?

In writing stories about these new teachers, I chose to have my writing represent both analysis and data presentation (Van Manen, 1990). My emphasis on story relates the research to the narrative inquiry described by Connelly and Clandinin (e.g., 1990). As the chapters reveal, the new teachers used our interviews as occasions to tell the stories most important to them at the time.

Polkinghorne (1988) indicated that story or narrative implied author, reader, point of view, plot, movement through time, dilemma, and dilemma resolution. Of these elements, two are troublesome to me. Plot suggests causality. Connelly and Clandinin (1990) use the work of Crites to claim that causality is an illusion: "A sequence of events looked at backward has the appearance of causal necessity and, looked at forward, has the sense of a teleological, intentional pull of the future. Thus . . . events tend to appear deterministically related" (p. 7). In place of causality, they suggest that narrative explanation derives from the whole, in which the interrelations of the parts can be viewed.

Another way to avoid a simple notion of causality is to use the language of biology rather than the language of physics. To make this shift, "the images of forces, trajectories, and direct causes are replaced with thinking . . . in terms of constant change and complex interdependencies" (Davis & Sumara, 1997, p. 109). Davis and Sumara described an alternative model of cognition, one that clearly helps to understand the stories of the new teachers.

Rather, the cognizing agent is recast as part of the context. As the learner learns, the context changes, simply because one of its components changes. Conversely, as the context changes, so does the very identity of the learner. Cast against a different set of circumstances, caught up in different sets of relationships, how we define ourselves and how we act is inevitably affected. And so, learning (and, similarly, teaching) cannot be understood in monologic terms: there is no direct causal, linear, fixable relationship among the various components of any community of practice. . . . Everything is inextricably intertwined with everything else. (1997, p. 111)

Dilemma is the second narrative element that gave me pause. The new teachers did not necessarily describe their lives by referring to dilemmas or dilemmas resolved. That is not to say there were no dilemmas—teaching is rife with dilemmas. Berlak and Berlak (1981), for example, used the notion of dilemma to explicate many of the tensions endemic to the enterprise of education. There is evidence of some of these dilemmas in the stories of the new teachers, but I did not focus on personal dilemmas resolved by the new teachers. I found helpful the distinctions made by Connelly and Clandinin (1986), who focused narrative not on problems or dilemmas, but on "the everyday business of schooling whether tense and problematic or routine and cyclic" (p. 11). I hoped to illustrate the new teachers' responses to the everyday aspects of schooling.

CHAPTER 2

Fred Fitting

Fred was a successful Cornell student who enjoyed his coursework. He was interviewed by Pat Kerr, a graduate student, in his junior year. His senior-year interview was done by Demetra Dentes, also a graduate student. These two students were older, experienced teachers, and excellent interviewers. I did all the other interviews with Fred. Fred consistently wrote out additional comments on the transcripts and drafts I sent him in order to elaborate his ideas or discuss his current thinking. As a freshman, Fred had taken an auto-tutorial introductory biology class, in which lectures and note taking were replaced by assigned readings and a workbook with objectives and study questions. Unlike some auto-tutorial courses, frequent examinations had to be completed by a deadline. The examinations were oral exams administered by the teaching assistants in the course. As a senior, Fred worked as an undergraduate teaching assistant in that same class and also observed in a middle school science class.

Fred did his student teaching in a magnet school that emphasized the development of the school as a learning community. He taught Regents biology and organized his own middle school science class. His cooperating teacher, Sam, was an energetic and experienced teacher who continually worked to improve his own teaching. Sam was beginning to replace lectures with student projects and extended assignments. In the middle school class, Fred attempted to duplicate the experiences he had had in the Adaptations course at the Shoals Marine Lab. The goal of the class was to have students develop their own experiments. I supervised his student teaching and taught the pre-student teaching seminar that year.

Fred found a teaching position in a small rural New York state school that had junior and senior high classes in one building. Although old, the building looked clean and well-maintained when I visited. Fred taught high school biology for both Regents and non-Regents students. In New York state there are mandated curricula for Regents classes, with end-of-year statewide tests. Students in non-Regents classes are considered less likely to go to college. Fred stayed at that school for the entire study, but later moved on. I gave him the surname Fitting, because he worked consciously to fit into that school, then chose the first name Fred because I like alliteration. I did not visit Fred during his first year of teaching because I was preparing for my tenure review. Fred had his own classroom, with a prep room attached to it. When I first visited, the classroom and prep room shelves still had materials that had accumulated for many years. By his third year, Fred had sorted out materials in the classroom but was still going through the things in the prep room. Some materials had been there a long time; one of the folders he threw out contained the student teaching evaluations of someone now a senior member of the faculty.

LEARNING

When Kerr asked Fred how he knew that he understood things in his college introductory biology class, Fred answered in terms specific to the procedures in the course.

Fred: You had a schedule—a unit [that lasted] about a week to 10 days. They would give you a number of pages to read and answer questions in the manual and assess whether you knew it or not. There would be an oral exam with a teaching assistant. [You would] sit down one on one with the TA and they would ask questions. . . . And they would also ask questions that would sort of tie in some information from other units, to keep up on what you have learned already and what you should be learning. And it was pretty good. If you actually didn't quite understand how something worked, and partial parts of how it did, you would sort of go through it with a TA during the exam. And they would lead you into the answer and a lot of times it would be quick, [that you'd learn it] right during the test.

Kerr: Did you like that?

Fred: I liked that a lot—I felt that was a lot better than a written exam because on a written exam you end up guessing . . . and the teacher cannot really see how you got the answer and if you understand anything of it. They can see if you understand some of it, or what is getting you into trouble. (Junior)

Fred felt it was important to make connections and to tie information together across units, and to use this information to figure out how things worked. A partial understanding meant that one had not figured out all the connections. This introductory biology course was key in helping Fred to learn to succeed in the university system. "Overall I guess I just felt it was a good course for me and sort of disciplined me to doing the work. . . . It didn't let you slack off." (Junior)

As a junior, Fred made no other references to strategies that he used to monitor his own developing understandings. He did say that the introductory biology course had helped him learn how to pick out necessary and important features from lectures in other courses that did not have the clearly delineated objectives and study guide used in the biology class, but he offered little detail about how he did this.

When he was a senior Demetra Dentes asked Fred to describe himself as a learner:

> I think I'm a better listener than I am anything. For discussions and things like that, I tend to be more on the quiet side, listening to what other people have to say . . . I feel that I have to get a little perspective from everybody. . . . What I initially think probably won't be a good idea because I still haven't considered what other people have said. . . . As a learner I'm better at assimilating other people's thoughts and ideas, then afterwards, like when I'm walking home from the class, I'll think about something I should have said, I could say now. (Senior)

This quote illustrates Fred's continuing concern about attending to and integrating information from different sources in order to form a full picture. He focused on learning within a classroom setting. Fred expressed no doubts about his learning; he did not castigate himself for being slow, for needing time to make sense of the material. As a senior Fred observed in a sixth-grade classroom and noted that using examples from everyday life helped students to grasp concepts in science.

When I interviewed Fred after his student teaching, he was enrolled in several science courses, including advanced mammalian physiology and introductory geology. He felt that it was now easier to do well in these courses because he could step back and look at biology and science as a whole, something he could not have done before. He felt he was able to apply principles, fit things into a big picture, and evaluate whether the topics that he was studying made sense to him. He felt that during his career at Cornell he had moved from memorizing and passing tests to applying, speculating, and relating. This quote and the next show how he articulated some of the metacognitive strategies he used to monitor his learning and how his work in teacher education contributed to his development as a learner:

> I guess what you just said sort of brings to mind a couple things about subject matter and just how I look at the world and my subject

matter differently now than I did 4 or 5 years ago when I first entered school here. I think that, through teaching and talking to students about the subject knowledge and about assimilating all my courses together [I am] taking a step back and sort of conceptualizing what biology is, not just a little piece by piece, but as a whole. And what science is as a whole. I think that, for example, courses which I took this past semester seem to fall into place a lot easier. (MAT)

When I asked Fred to describe himself as a learner, he illustrated his thinking process, giving his internal dialogue:

Again, trying to fit things into what's there already, relating them to what's there. . . . For example, in biology I'm trying to relate why a kidney does this and that. I think about diffusion . . . and what this drug does. "Okay, it's going to block so and so, so that way diffusion can't take place."
   I think as a learner now I . . . listen to what the professor's saying and I try to say, "Okay, how does that fit with what I have already? And does that make sense?" So sort of go through it step by step sometimes. . . . Just stick to the basic principles involved. . . . It's just sort of . . . a cascade often, I think. It just leads to more and more things and different situations. . . . If it doesn't make sense, then try to follow up and figure out why it's not fitting or what piece am I missing or what's not quite right inside here or why can't I make the connection. Not be afraid to. (MAT)

I wonder now what Fred would have said if I had asked him about being afraid. A year after this interview, when he was a first-year teacher, Fred read a draft of a preliminary paper I wrote and responded to it, but made no explicit mention of anxiety, although he again noted that it took him time to learn.
   I asked Fred how he told if students understood. He noted it was hard, but that students usually got excited when something clicked with them and then could ask questions that were relevant and appropriate. You also might tell from their written work, although they could just guess at their answers. He added:

But if you design questions that sort of make students put together several different things from different parts of the book then, I think [whether] they make the correct linkages is a key. . . . If they can go back to some underlying principles like diffusion or something like that. (MAT)

In this interview Fred was grappling with how to determine when someone understood. He continued to question the validity of written tests to determine understanding, preferring an interactive setting and discussion to determine true student understanding. It could be that he was beginning to sense one of the uncertainties of teaching (see, for example, Feiman-Nemser & Featherstone, 1992). However, he seemed to attribute this uncertainty to the format of the evaluation rather than to an unavoidable uncertainty.

BIOLOGY

As a junior, it was clear that Fred loved biology classes. He recounted that his college introductory biology class had changed his way of thinking about the world. Biology provided, for him, knowledge of mechanisms that explained observable phenomena, phenomena that he could now see in a new way. Pat Kerr had asked about a powerful learning experience he recalled from biology.

Fred: Well, I remember in my first semester of intro bio it convinced me that I liked it, that biology was what I really wanted to do. I think just knowing how things work, some anatomy and the muscle system, how they work. And I remember looking at my hand and saying, "Wow, I know what happens when I do this and exactly what is going on." I think that was probably something I remember.
Pat: Why did that grab you?
Fred: I'm not sure, I guess just you take for granted simple things you do everyday and yet people have no idea of what goes on. And all of a sudden you ask the question like when you were small and all of a sudden you know how and you don't take it for granted as much as you used to. (Junior)

Fred completed a general biology major and as a senior remarked he had gained an overview of the whole field of biology at the expense of taking advanced courses in any one area. "So I don't know what I'm actually best in. I do pretty well in a little bit of everything." His concern about his major appears to relate more to his abilities rather than to the nature of the discipline of biology. Now I wish Dentes had followed up on his comment.

Fred's work as an undergraduate teaching assistant in the introductory biology course he loved was important for him because it helped him understand better the topics covered and their interrelations. He clearly viewed this course as representing the central ideas in biology. His response also suggests he initially had relied on at least some memorization to pass the course as a freshman:

> Going through the material a second time . . . reinforced a lot of the concepts and basic ideas of biology for me. . . . And now I see like Unit 1 through 10, now I see how they fit together, whereas when I was a freshman taking the course it was like, "Okay, I've got to get through Unit 1, do the work for Unit 1, cram it all in." . . . When you've got to teach it, you could definitely see the flow of one unit to the next. (Senior)

Fred viewed the structure of biology as a coherent system. "I still think that I feel strongly about things being part of a system and that everything is related." (Senior)

Although Fred acknowledged that the field of biology changed over time, he did not stress this view in his discussions of teaching and learning. Fred pointed out that he'd observed that secondary students thought that scientific knowledge was absolute, not tentative. "I don't think the students know what science entails . . . it's just all these facts and stuff to learn as opposed to this ongoing thing." (MAT)

Fred's view of biology as a coherent, interrelated, and explainable system persisted. In the MAT interview, I had mentioned something about needing to be flexible as a teacher, and he discussed what that meant for him.

> So I think flexible in the sense where I'm always trying to think of those underlying examples which are always there and . . . and present them in numerous different ways. . . . I guess just realizing that most everything is going to underlie and relate to other things. . . . Thinking about as many connections as you can and presenting them to students so that they say, "Ah, aha, so that's why this does this and that and the other thing!" (MAT)

LABORATORY INSTRUCTION

When Kerr asked Fred about a favorite lab exercise from introductory college biology, Fred's response emphasized his view that inquiry involved the manipulation and control of variables to create situations that would provide meaningful comparisons. He preferred this over prescribed cookbook labs that provided no opportunity for thought.

Pat: Which one did you like to do the most of the labs?

Fred: The first semester we did a basic physiology lab on cardiopulmo-
nary [function] on a person and we had to design the lab ourselves
and expand it and see how exercise affected pulse rate and lung
capacity and things like that. I thought that was interesting. [Some
did] simple exercises or maybe drank a few cups of coffee and saw
what the rate was and blood pressure.

Pat: What did you like about doing that?

Fred: We could be sort of creative on our own. We weren't restricted, it
wasn't a cookbook lab step by step—do this and do this. [You]
would have to think about it and what your objective and goal was
and start doing it. A lot of the labs you just open the book and read
it and do the exercises and that's it.

Pat: So you think you learn more by doing this?

Fred: I think so, yeah.

Pat: Other than just pulmonary—

Fred: Yeah, in a sense some research methods because we were on our
own, to see what we want to do and what we want to find out and
how we are going to do that—what's going to be a good control,
how are you going to control this factor and so forth. (Junior)

During Fred's senior-year interview he amplified his earlier description of a good lab and included more detail on the importance of having a
testable hypothesis,

> You could go in and look at one little aspect that you find interest-
> ing, and see if you are able to design something. You could see how
> labs are going to have to eliminate variables here and here and you
> have a control, and you're going to have to design a procedure
> which is going to look at the goal that you have in mind, or the
> variable you have in mind. (Senior)

During his student teaching, Fred had hoped to have his middle school
students investigate something they were interested in, to develop their
own hypotheses and procedures to test them. Some students were more
successful than others, but many had problems, often because they investigated something about which they knew little. In the semester after student teaching, Fred took a curriculum course and analyzed one of the BSCS
curricula. Until this time he had not realized that there were developed
curricula that presented science not just as a body of facts, but as "a thinking process where people ask questions and then gather information in

order to see if they can answer that question with the information. And that science isn't static, it's dynamic and keeps on going." (MAT)

PRACTICE AS A NEW TEACHER—YEAR TWO

During his second year of teaching I spent a spring day at the school with Fred. I met with the principal, who was very enthusiastic about Fred and his energy and hard work, but noted that, as with many new teachers, the percentage of Fred's biology students who had passed the Regents exam the previous year was lower than usual. The principal was confident that a larger percentage would pass in the current year. Classes I saw tended to be relatively small, with 20 students on average. On the day I observed, Fred spent the class time doing standard teaching activities. He lectured to present content, using the overhead projector, while students took notes. He frequently interspersed his lecture with questions to the students to check that they understood and he answered questions from them. The tone of his class was warm and relaxed, and students seemed to relate well to him. Fred's pleasant and well-managed classroom facilitated content coverage. Fred and I held our conversations during his planning periods and lunch.

Scheduling of labs was a problem for Fred at this school. The school administration had resisted pleas from the whole science department to have double periods for science classes scheduled on alternate days to use for laboratory teaching, a common practice in New York State. Fred's lab sections were held at the end of the day and were only one class period long. In addition, students were assigned to lab sections from more than one class, so Fred could not form lab groups who also could work during lecture time. The scheduling gave Fred little opportunity to provide anything other than the most routine of exercises in lab, exercises that focused on content learning rather than on science processes. Fred could see no way to plan any exploratory kinds of laboratory activities. "I barely have time to pass labs out, prep for it, do it, and then clean up. And then we have very little time to debrief."

Fred's school district endorsed the New York State-endorsed Outcomes Based Instruction (OBI), in which outcomes are spelled out and tested for explicitly. Students who do not do well on a test are allowed to study more and take a repeat test on the sections they did not pass. Fred was one of a group of teachers who were revising their courses to become outcomes-based and had attended a workshop and been given support from New York State funds over the previous summer for OBI curriculum development work. As Fred explained it, the outcomes-based approach did not attend to laboratory teaching or inquiry and did not emphasize the tentative nature of science knowledge. Designing the materials to support the OBI approach was a time-consuming activity for Fred, who was the only biology teacher in the school and so had no colleagues with whom to work. However, the New York State Regents curriculum prescribed the content to be covered, so Fred did not need to spend time deciding on the content to be covered.

Fred described the OBI approach and how he modified these procedures for the non-Regents students, allowing them to get credit even when they did not reach the criterion score on a retest (some, he felt, would never reach this score).

Fred: We do retests in here, and I divide the tests up into sections so that there's five questions for each section. If you get an 80 or 100 on either section, you don't you have to redo that section.

Deb: Oh, mastery grading.

Fred: Yeah. Mastery—learning. And that old outcomes-based instruction. I've never really bothered writing the outcomes for the class, but the tests are divided into outcomes. Like Outcome One this last test we had was energy transfer. And the information it dealt with was glucose. Glucose is changed to ATP, and energy is released and the cell uses that. So I have five questions dealing with that information. And they have to get four of the five right or they have to retest. (Year Two)

Fred still was anxious that students be able to apply principles and reason through an example. For example, we discussed one test question that I read.

Deb: "Which metabolic waste is correctly matched with the process that produces it?" That's interesting. (I did not read out loud the choices on this multiple choice examination.)

Fred: That's an old Regents exam question. So this was trying to get them recognizing that proteins are broken down and urea is a waste product. "Is that true, does that match up?" In this case it does. "Do you get carbon dioxide?" . . . . So if you didn't get 80% on outcome number two, you have to do this problem set, in class, that following day.

Deb: Okay, so the correctives are—more short answer.

Fred: Short answer, trying to get the students back to the notes, taking a look at the notes, getting the basics again so that they have the material to answer questions like this. And I also take a look at what question they missed. If a lot of kids missed it, I'll make sure I have a question very similar to that on the outcome. (Year Two)

Fred's description of one student further illustrated his hope that students would think for themselves and apply the material learned. His description of the student reveals Fred's fondness for the student and his feeling that his school did not nourish or value students' thinking independently:

> Timothy is considered, I think, by a lot of teachers sort of a trouble maker. He's said to me this is his favorite class. And he doesn't miss in this class and he's *really* interested in it. He's got so many questions. Thousands. . . . He often stays after class for a couple minutes and talks and tries to figure out something. Comes up with—weird things. Very creative, all the time doing something or showing me something he does. A lot of teachers don't take him as being intelligent. Or just, I don't know. He strikes me as very intelligent. If he had the opportunity to go to a good school, he'd do phenomenally. (Year Two)

Fred said he had faced problems in his first teaching year when he tried to include essay questions on exams and use means other than multiple choice tests to assess student learning. In his second year, his exams were all multiple choice questions. I didn't follow up on these comments in our conversations but focused instead on understanding his current course organization. Fred was, as he put it, playing the game by teaching in the way valued by the school, using the same format the science coordinator used. Fred was teaching in a way that it was felt would help the most students pass the Regents examination.

Fred was working hard to identify reasonable outcomes for the course and to relate these to unit and lesson outcomes. As far as I could tell, the outcomes did not include attention to students' ways of thinking in and about science. While he was doing this work—and it took a great deal of organization to plan the examinations, review sheets, and follow-up examinations—I think Fred also was developing his own vision of the connections in the curriculum that he was teaching, and was learning about his students' needs.

PRACTICE AS A NEW TEACHER—YEAR THREE

In his third year, Fred was still working on implementing an OBI approach, with little support. "And we meet about once a month. . . . I don't know what we do there. I show my things, 'That's nice.'"

In the classes I observed, Fred performed like an experienced and very accomplished teacher, using a well-orchestrated approach to lecturing. He prepared outlines for the lecture, passed them out to students, and then used overheads of the outlines. As he went through the material, he wrote the content on the overhead and the students filled in the handout. He began each new section of the lecture with a general question to students, asking them to think about the material before he presented it for note taking. He remained open to student questions and comments during his lecturing. More important, he regularly interrupted the lecture and note-taking process by moving from the overhead projector to a blackboard, where he would scrawl a few things. He told students not to take notes when he did this, but to listen, discuss, and review, and make connections across units and topics.

Deb: That's a nice use of board; it differentiates functions.
Fred: Sure. It's not note taking, but, "Let's listen and try to get this for a second."
Deb: "You've had this before, you should know this." So you're tying up bits and pieces.
Fred: Sure. It took them a little bit [to learn the system], but then they started to get it. (Year Three)

This strategy also allowed Fred to signal to his students that there were principles that would apply across units and that would help explain the specific phenomenon studied.

Fred reported that he was generally happy in his third year of work at the school. Fred believed that his students were better than last year. He was continuing to use Outcomes Based Instruction and had made the objectives public in an effort to help students study, although he had not yet rewritten his outcome statements to reflect better his concerns that students make connections and apply principles. Fred felt he needed to present the Regents-mandated material, but worked to find a way to alleviate the need for constant student note taking. He also was taking action to help the students learn how to study and organize their work, realizing that they needed explicit instruction in these areas. He was trying to cover the mandated content in less time and more efficiently in order to create for himself a chance to do more inquiry during class time.

Fred: They're [the school] still big on this Outcomes Based Instruction. Which this sheet [of objectives] is an example of. Other teachers don't do this, but I came out with these sheets for the kids because I found that last year students just didn't have very many organizational skills as far as taking notes. And I wanted to streamline the note-taking process so I could . . . use some class time for labs, eventually.

For example, tomorrow I'll start the class and we'll do a 10-minute review like, "Okay, take out a piece of paper and let's think about what we did yesterday." . . . And we'll get through the notes, and have some discussion and do some worksheets and do some problem solving with it. And then we have our test.

Deb: They certainly seem to be taking notes assiduously.

Fred: Yeah, I've got a really good group this year and . . . all but two students passed the midterm. The midterm, I thought, was pretty thorough on what we covered so far. So that was encouraging. I think one reason is because they have everything, it's right there, and they have it and they're more organized than some of the kids were last year. Because last year I worked with the overhead, but they put it on their own piece of paper. And who knows where it ended up. . . . I want to incorporate some of the things that we did this summer, for the Environment and Computing Workshop [at Cornell]. (Year Three)

I commented on the ease with which Fred referred to the course material in his lecture and discussion, since he recalled just when they had studied some material, reviewed what they did with it then, related it to what they were doing now, and referred to work they would soon be doing. He agreed that he really knew the Regents curriculum now, and said, "Like if I had my eyes closed in this room I can sort of move around it with no problem. I know what's going to be there, and I can draw some examples . . . from the outside that they can understand." (Year Three)

We spoke more explicitly about his approach to teaching in our third-year conversations. The driving force, he acknowledged, was helping students to pass the Regents exam, which was crucial to gaining tenure. His hope to have students make connections was something that was peripheral. He described his work:

[I'm] at a point now, mostly fine tuning teaching them facts and straightforward things. And on the side trying to get them to put it all together. . . . This is a good method for teaching all the stuff that's going to be on the Regents, the details. It's just lenticles, lenticles, lenticles, til you're blue in the face. And every time I say, "Holes in stems," you'll say, "Lenticle." (Year Three)

Fred knew that he was adjusting his teaching to meet the demands of his school. He was still working to develop ways to incorporate more of the lab work he considered important. In his third year of teaching I felt comfortable enough to push a bit and asked Fred what he would do differently in an ideal teaching situation. Fred said he probably would include most of the same information that was in the Regents curriculum but would change the testing from an emphasis on memorization to a concern with questions that required students to think about and apply knowledge and to develop explanations of the mechanisms operating. He was specific, too, about the need for students to relate course content to their worlds outside class:

> I'm more interested in seeing how they get the big picture and how things fit together . . . not just that the lenticles are a little hole in the side of the stem. Just know the fact that plants have to get energy, so they do this process like we do, respiration, so that means they must need oxygen too. And then, it's relatively simple how they get it, little holes. . . . How can the kids use information from this course *really* to make a difference, to make them aware of something that's outside. (Year Three)

I asked Fred about the tension between his ideals and the current situation. He felt that once he proved his ability to help students perform well on the Regents exams, he could then move to do more alternative teaching. At present, he did not really feel he had much choice in how he taught.

Fred: The whole thing's like a transition thing.
Deb: Do you think that's inevitable as a developing teacher?
Fred: I think so, given the system we're in now. . . . So the first couple years, like I said last year, playing the game.
Deb: What kind of personal cost is there to that? Have you felt any personal cost?
Fred: Yeah. I, I mean . . . I like the information we teach, I don't like being bound into having to teach the kids in this methodical way. . . . I realize I have to do that first. Sometimes I feel guilty about doing it, like saying, "Geez, I know, they have to know it and the way I do it I know I teach them how to know it." But then I take a look and wonder, because what are they really getting out of the course? And it's not a lot. So how do we make that transition into doing some of the same stuff but still learning more on top of that, and putting that together? So that's where I'm at now. 'Cause I think, I'll be here next year, I have no worry about that. (Year Three)

SUMMARY

Fred's ideas about learning remained relatively constant. He focused on making connections, understanding mechanisms and underlying principles, and applying content to the world around him. Fred commented that it took him time to put together information from different sources, but he seemed to have assumed that the information would all fit together. This faith and his confidence in himself supported the systematic approach he took to learning biology content, even though it took time. His experiences tutoring in the auto-tutorial biology course helped him to see the story line of the course, the logical connections across topics, and he mastered the Regents curriculum that he taught in the same way.

His view of learning thus fit with his conception of biology as a coherent field of study in which there was an overall big picture into which individual facts and concepts would fit. He occasionally mentioned that biological knowledge was incomplete and being added to, but did not make this central to his teaching.

Fred was not critical of the laboratory exercises he had done at Cornell. His favorite labs involved experimental investigations, but his student teaching attempt to teach students to investigate scientifically was not too successful because he had not paid enough attention to students' background knowledge. As a teacher he did not feel he had the opportunity to do investigations in lab sections because of insufficient time.

After his student teaching, Fred had some awareness that it was hard to determine a student's comprehension, but when he began using the OBI framework he focused on student performance on multiple choice exams to indicate success because these were the indicators valued in his school. Fred worked hard to implement the OBI approach favored by his school. The procedures that were part of the OBI approach fit with Fred's systematic approach to learning and his experiences in the Cornell auto-tutorial course. Fred had not figured out a way to provide oral exams in his teaching, but the use of the review and retesting did allow Fred to provide his students with an exam that could be a learning experience. I did not push Fred or share some of my concerns about OBI during our interviews in his second year of teaching. In our third-year interview, Fred indicated that he had helped his students succeed at the game that was important in the school. They became better at taking notes and passing exams, and they performed acceptably on the Regents examination. In his third year he was much more explicitly critical of the teaching that he was doing, stating that much of his work simply fostered memorization of terms, even though he tried to show students how to make connections and apply material across units.

In reading a draft of the full case study after he had left his first school for a position elsewhere, Fred commented that what was important was, "What can I do so that students get more (not content) out of a course?" rather than "Can I get this student past the exam?" When he read his views of learning as a junior, he wrote: "This is what I would like to see in some of my students. It is very exciting for me when I have a student get really into the topic."

CHAPTER 3

Pat Green

Pat was in the same cohort as Fred Fitting, and the two were good friends. Pat also was interviewed by graduate students Kerr and Dentes for the first and second year of the study, and I did the rest of the interviews and observations. Prior to beginning coursework TESM, Pat had worked with some youngsters from low-income families in the area. When she interviewed for admission into the TESM program, she was quite adamant that she would not give up this work, even though she also was going to have to do field work for the TESM program. I called her Pat to honor Pat Kerr, the graduate student from whom I learned so much. Green reflects Pat's continual striving to grow.

In her senior year Pat did her field work with a local middle school teacher who considered himself a conceptual change teacher and allowed his students many opportunities to develop their own ideas.

I taught the pre-student teaching seminar and supervised Pat's student teaching in a rural high school where she taught both Regents and non-Regents biology classes. Pat worked with a teacher who began each year with the activities for the whole year planned and scheduled. This teacher used lectures and lab exercises to present the content and help students learn the material needed to pass the Regents exam. After graduating, Pat took a junior high teaching position in her hometown in a southern state. The principal of her former junior high school had heard that she was looking for a job in the area and called her in to interview. During her first year of teaching, Pat taught eighth-grade physical science classes to students in tracked classes. As with Fred, I did not visit Pat during her first year of teaching. Pat reported that it had been a hard year. In her second year, Pat taught seventh-grade biology classes, and in her third year returned to teaching eighth-grade physical science, but this time in heterogeneous classes. Pat had her own classroom, which was decorated with student work, commercial posters, and other materials.

LEARNING

As a junior, Pat recalled being scared when she began college at Cornell, unsure how she would compare with other students. She had spent a year abroad after high school and found the experience significant. She said she realized one day "this idea that suddenly I knew absolutely nothing and there was so much over there I could learn, there wasn't a step I could take without seeing something brand new."

As a high school student she had liked to learn but felt she had not been into academics. Before coming to Cornell, Pat said, she had realized that she needed to be more responsible for her own learning, even though courses would provide her with structure for learning. She felt learning was an active process. "What I learn here is what I learn and there's nobody else, so I have to do that for myself. It's not going to be handed to me on a silver plate for the rest of my life."

Although Pat felt learning required effort, she thought she learned some things without realizing it. For example, she'd realized she had learned a lot in introductory biology class because in advanced biology classes, "I used a lot of things I learned" and "would attack a problem" differently. Learning "tiny batches" of content was much less important than learning to ask questions and think about the content.

Although as a junior Pat didn't describe strategies that she used when learning, she did feel that the teaching assistants in courses helped validate her understanding. "Maybe it came from talking with the TAs, one on one. And having them listen to you."

When she was interviewed in her senior year, Pat considered that developing a sense of efficacy was most important. Developing a sense of efficacy went beyond merely learning the content. Pat was not clear about the actual content that needed to be learned. She felt it was important "that they [students] leave their class with the feeling that they could learn it on their own now, that they could continue on their own, and that they have enough of a base to keep on learning."

She still believed one result of real learning was the ability to apply the material learned and she again demonstrated a belief that at least part of learning occurs without awareness because "they're gonna get from the class a lot of things they don't realize. I know that happens to me. Just things you start to use and you can't figure out where they came from."

When Pat was a junior she had done clinical interviews to learn novices' explanations for water boiling. She attributed her interviewees' inability to reason through the situation to a lack of confidence or self-efficacy, rather than to their lack of requisite knowledge. Perhaps because she had learned the requisite knowledge without being aware of it, she assumed the other Cornell students whom she interviewed also would have learned this content but just had failed to apply it. As she put it, the Cornell students she interviewed had

> all sorts of different ideas about what heat did to molecules which, to me, seemed strange because that's a very basic concept. It seemed to me that students would realize that it just makes molecules move faster. [These interviews were] very interesting because the interviewees were very capable of figuring out what was going on but they just didn't realize it. (Senior)

Pat's concern with interviewees who were reluctant to speculate may well have been shaped by memories of her own development as a learner. She speculated that students often believed

> that what you think isn't really worthwhile. That's the way I felt as a learner and I don't know how you would convey that to a group of students, that what they know and what they're learning at that very instant is all they need to know to figure something out on their own. But for me I didn't realize, I didn't see where this tiny bit of knowledge fit in. (Senior)

In her interviews with other Cornell students, Pat observed different patterns of learning and thinking, and realized these differences were important for a teacher to see:

> Some of them it helped to use drawing, on paper. That was important for me to see. "Okay, well some people want paper." Other people said "No, no I don't want to draw, it doesn't help me." And they were very adamant. (Senior)

As a senior Pat referred to concepts as those ideas that link together details. She knew that most of her learning was sufficient for passing tests as they were commonly written, but felt that she had problems linking things together on those exam questions that called for integration. She explained:

> I have a hard time knowing what the concepts I should be learning are, because I learned the details. I can pass the tests well, but when

they ask me one of those big questions at the end of the test which supposedly links everything together, I can't link it. (Senior)

In the semester after student teaching, Pat took some courses with a colleague in the TESM program, Fred Fitting. For the first time in our conversations, Pat supplied detail about the processes she used to learn. It is obvious that she gained confidence through her work with Fred, who was quite comfortable when he could not quickly figure things out and who had developed an explicit study strategy. Pat also indicated how lack of confidence in the past had contributed to her use of less successful learning strategies when she was confused.

Pat: Now, that sort of thing [class problem] I would have never even bothered trying to really do it. I would have tried memorizing the pattern . . . [I would have] looked at a bunch of different examples seeing what did they usually do in a case like that. "Is this case like this case? Okay, I'll do the same thing."

Deb: So, looking for the algorithm?

Pat: Yes. So that's been a big thing this semester, with physiology. Trying to figure out *why* I was doing that, not just because the other problem is done the same way. 'Cause Fred works that way very much. He doesn't go on. He doesn't get through his assignments nearly as quickly as I do. (I laugh) But . . . he figures them *out*. Because that sort of thing is intriguing to him, it's not nearly as traumatic, to him. So I think I've learned a lot from working with him. And that's been good. (MAT)

I asked her whether she had thought, when she was looking for the algorithms, that she was doing her best.

Pat: I thought I was doing the best job possible, yes. But I didn't think I was getting it. 'Cause I put in the time, but I put in repetitive time. . . . I really wasn't taking it into my own hands, to figure out what was going on. Out of fear and disinterest.

Deb: Was it fear of failure?

Pat: Fear that when I turned to that other page it was going to look just as wild as this first page. (MAT)

Pat's increased confidence, shaped by working with Fred, enabled her to work better toward taking responsibility for her understanding of science content. Although she spoke freely about needing to develop confidence, in this same interview, Pat expressed a realization about learning to teach that required great self-confidence.

> It's a wonderful feeling that I've been allowed to . . . organize what you, what we've discussed in class—and what we've written in class. I've been organizing what's important about those experiences for myself. Every once in a while I wonder about whether I've got something completely wrong. (laughs) If I have a very messed up big picture. But since I don't figure anybody else has that great an idea on the big picture, it's not [a problem]. (MAT)

This realization is daunting to those who expect to find in teacher education programs infallible techniques and guaranteed methods for teaching. Pat acknowledged the ambiguity of teaching and claimed her ability to make sense of it for herself. She said that one reason that she was comfortable with her realization was that learning could often be serendipitous. Part of the realization stemmed from her recognition that she learned things without being aware she had learned. Part of the realization was based on her observations of the learners with whom she had worked. She pointed out:

> Everyone's mind works differently. And in different situations. So many of your ideas, or your organization of your ideas, seems to be coincidental, sometimes, for me. A lot of times, something clicks in my brain, but it could very well click due to a haphazard experience. (MAT)

When I asked her how she could tell if a learner really understood something, she replied quickly that she "hadn't figured that out yet." After we both laughed, and she'd started to leave, she returned and mentioned that giving open-ended writing assignments did help determine how students understood things. Again, she accepted the lack of certainty that pervades teaching. Parallel to what she expressed as a senior, Pat seemed to accept that not all students would develop ideas at the same time and in the same ways, and reported that she could enjoy watching this process. "And I still every once in a while get a real kick, and I'm just *shocked* that they got that particular idea out of the lesson I gave. But, it's more interesting to me now than just [thinking], 'What are they doing wrong?'" (MAT)

BIOLOGY

In her junior-year interview Pat said that learning biology was more than the acquisition of new facts, that it also should help the learner grasp the mechanisms behind everyday events. Pat said one danger in courses that presented too general a picture of biology was that students would not question material. The following quote also suggests her view of learning as being a process that is never completed:

> When you go outside and look at a tree or something, you have a better idea of how it works. . . . Because lots of times in introductory courses you just get a general overview and I wouldn't even think to ask questions beyond that. But all of a sudden they're telling me this and this and that's making me more interested in getting more particulars to find out just why this does this and when you finally do know, or think you know, that's even one more reason why. (Junior)

Pat's concern to understand fully also appeared when she talked about using concept maps (Novak & Gowin, 1984) as a way to show relations among concepts and thus gain an overview of the content in the introductory biology class. Friends of hers had done concept mapping in the course, and she liked the purpose for using concept maps, but she found them frustrating to do "because there were too many of the concepts that I didn't understand what they meant." (Junior)

In her senior-year interview, Pat stressed the importance of stimulating learners' interest in biology and awareness of their existing knowledge. Her commitment clearly was shaped by her experiences with the youngsters whom she tutored for several years while a student at Cornell.

Pat: Because the only reason you're learning from a book is so that you can think about things in a bigger sense anyway. So it really does reflect how I feel about learning in science. Because so many of the students I've worked with don't read well, don't give a hoot for a book. What's important is not so much what they can learn from a book but what they already know themselves. And to get them interested in that.

Deme: How would [your students] assess their own learning?

Pat: I would guess the most important thing, for them, is if they want to learn these concepts again they could. I would suggest that a lot of the concepts they're not going to remember—or maybe concepts but not nitty gritty details. (Senior)

Having worked as a senior with a middle school teacher who let students work at figuring things out, Pat noted that there were times when the students would not grasp concepts, but she, like the teacher, did not seem concerned about it. She recognized and accepted the unpredictability of learning. "We played with that [idea] for about an hour and the students got closer and closer. But, actually, that concept they never hit. But some concepts they *do* come up with on their own, they *do* figure out." (Senior)

Some of Pat's other comments as a senior reflected another dimension to the particular/big picture tension. This dimension, one I had not thought of before, related to her views about the curriculum. I wonder, indeed, how many science students share her beliefs. Pat said that earlier she had not thought that what she knew was worthwhile because she did not realize its generality until she had taken several biology courses. She did not, though, consider these ideas important to all of biology. She explained:

> Going over the same things and realizing, "Hey, these *are* the basic concepts . . . I can base my thoughts on. . . . One conflict I have now that—and nobody else seems to have had—but I went through those chapters in biology and I didn't know I was getting a really good overall view of [biology]. I had no idea these concepts applied all over. I thought, "Okay, we've gone through 10 chapters. I'm sure there must be Chapters 11 through 125 still to go." . . . It wasn't until I'd had to take the course [any introductory biology course] three or four times since my high school biology that it's occurring to me that maybe there isn't that much more outside of what they're teaching. Now, I don't accept that completely, I know there are all sorts of ideas. (Senior)

After her student teaching, which was devoted to training high school students to pass the Regents examination, Pat stated why she felt that learning biology was important. She loved biology because

> it makes my life so much more interesting. . . . It enriches your life. . . . Biology can allow you to get excited about real things, if you want. Biology could provide a cheap and harmless hobby so that you never really have to be bored. (MAT)

She contrasted her view to that of other students in the TESM program who also had completed student teaching. "Everybody else is talking about teaching this concept, that concept. For me, I think the most important thing is to get people interested, because that enriches your life." (MAT)

LABORATORY INSTRUCTION

Pat's favorite lab in the freshman biology class had not been a lab that focused on experimentation but rather a cockroach dissection that opened her eyes to some of the complexities she had ignored previously.

I liked that because there was a whole world inside all these in-
sects . . . and it gave me a chance to see that and realize how neat
that was and it was training my mind to go deeper into things and
look at the smaller and smaller things that go into making it up . . .
to my surprise. (Junior)

When Kerr asked her, Pat felt that she'd learned about doing science
investigations from lab, but offered few details:

I can design an experiment and have a lot of confidence in using
different equipment. I have an idea of not just asking the superficial
questions that you ask when you first get in, but asking more and
more. (Junior)

In her senior-year interview, Dentes pointed out to Pat that lab work
was a large part of introductory biology and asked her why she thought it
was emphasized. Pat's response indicated she conceived of labs as having
several different functions, only one of which was to give students the
chance to engage in inquiry. Her standard critique of scripted lab activities analyzed both the possible intent of the activity and her reactions to it.
She also maintained that activities should have some personal meaning and
purpose, which could result when the abstract notions were made concrete
by lab experiences. She noted that labs provided a change of routine, making the content memorable:

I always assumed [lab] was a consequence of [designers] trying to
make it relate more to your own life, so you can see it happening.
You can remember the experience, for one thing, because you're
going to remember something that was different from your average
class. Also, I think it is assuming that if students see it happen
they'll have a better idea of how to figure it out on their own. That
didn't work with me! I just read instructions, and did it like I was
cooking a recipe. It just seemed to me it was an experiment that had
been done thousands and thousands of times and really wasn't
used by real scientists. I didn't see any personalization of it and I
didn't feel it put me on an equal plane with biology researchers. I
had no feeling that the research was important. (Senior)

At another point, Pat elaborated an idea about the importance of learning about scientific laboratory work. She felt it was important for students
to do some of their own laboratory work and it was also important for students to learn about the actual people doing science work:

Because that way you can tell what these guys who have written articles were going through. And it's really neat when they start telling you about these people and you don't feel they are someplace else that is miles away, but they are actually from nearby. (Senior)

I have always considered that having practicing scientists visit secondary schools or bringing pupils into scientific laboratories were activities that actually made youngsters more confused about science. Pat's responses, though, enabled me to comprehend a real value to such activities. Pat said that when she read articles or references to textbook content in *Time* magazine or heard lectures by researchers, that she fully realized that the content of biology was being developed at present, by real people, and felt that the work was therefore personalized. Too many of the labs she had done neither enabled her to feel much connection nor helped her to feel the work had any significance.

Pat did not claim that there was one unique scientific reasoning. Instead, she felt that thinking scientifically was synonymous with thinking critically and "the other part of it would be just the open mind, to look at everything and be very creative in the questions you ask." (Senior)

In her MAT interview Pat again said that she didn't think there was any method peculiar to science; rather, the scientific method involved thinking critically, being open-minded, and using the thought processes necessary for any critical thought. As before, she did not elaborate on what these processes were.

PRACTICE AS A NEW TEACHER—YEAR TWO

During her first year teaching, Pat had taught 3 eighth-grade, lower-track science courses, with laboratories, and one period of a nonscience course. She said that her second year teaching all seventh-grade heterogeneous classes was much easier; "these guys are cake." Pat was excited that there were five new science teachers who had taught 4 years or less, were very "gung-ho," and worked together a lot.

When I observed Pat in her second year, I watched an open-ended lesson with several goals. Over dinner the night before, when I had asked what she was planning to do the next day, Pat joked that she wasn't really sure but that she'd think of something. After observing her first class, I could tell she had planned carefully. She had library books and materials selected and arranged in the classroom. Over the day, as she repeated the lesson, she modified the instructions she gave to the students to ensure that the activities met her goals. She had structured the class activity to avoid lecturing on the material and to help students find new information and combine that with material they had studied previously. The assignment required each group of students to pick an animal, find information about it, then design a plaque to describe important things about the animal. Each group then had to explain their plaque to the rest of the class. This exercise was in preparation for a trip they would take to the local zoo in a few days. When I asked Pat about her plan after I observed a few classes, her rationale for the activities included motivation for eighth graders, learning how to find and synthesize information, and learning how to present information. There were central biological topics covered in her lesson, and Pat wanted her students to become engaged with them. She structured the work to match her students' needs and interests. The activity involved groupwork, reading, using references and prior knowledge, drawing, and presenting to the class as a whole. She elaborated:

> There were, I think, three objects. One . . . I wanted them to have written their own plaques. . . . I've found, with these kids, if they've done it their way once, and then they see someone else's way, especially like an adult way, they'll immediately compare and usually criticize. But at least they're reading and they're interested in finding what someone else has provided for them.
> The other thing I wanted was to expose them to some other animals before we get to the zoo. I didn't want to just sit up there and talk about all the different animals that belong to the different biomes. I just wanted to see what they could get. And a third object was to go through how they can get information from a book, having been told we want that information that's on the board. I want them to be able to look through the book and get the information. I wanted to see if they did any better today, having done [a similar exercise] already. (Year Two)

Pat explicated the relationships between various factors that affected student work, and continued to believe that nearly everyone could learn:

> In fact, most of my students are capable, if they really wanted to learn. I think it's more a degree of how their personality makes them either interested or not interested in learning it. Some of them are so driven. And then, of course, their personality's shaped by whether it comes to them easily or not. And if it does, they tend to push themselves. And if it doesn't, they don't. (Year Two)

PRACTICE AS A NEW TEACHER—YEAR THREE

When I visited Pat in her third year of teaching, she was again teaching eighth-grade physical science, but in heterogeneous classes. Since she had taught seventh grade the year before, she had many of the same students and found it to be a positive experience. I was, of course, interested in learning how Pat compared teaching biology with teaching physical science. Her contrast reveals one of the difficulties of teaching biology, the lack of easy demonstrations of phenomena.

Deb: What's it like teaching physical science?
Pat: I love it.
Deb: How come? Rather than bio?
Pat: You can do so much. Easy, easy fun, and funny things to do with it. And, I don't think it's harder for the students to understand. . . . But there just seem so many ways that I can involve them. Like, right now I don't give homework, written homework. All the homeworks are take-home labs. And I'm developing just a series of little magic tricks that they take home. And it has a little article that usually goes with it. And then it has, "Do this magic trick, and see how it works." And then I have some questions I've added on . . . to explain how this demo worked. (Year Three)

Pat continued to have as a major goal that students become intrigued and interested and that they realize that scientific understandings are generated by people. I asked her about the wing design exercise I had observed.

Deb: What would you want to see that they had gotten out of this lesson? The whole thing on Bernoulli's principle?
Pat: Foremost and above all, it's just interest. To actually think, "Oh, there's someone out there who had to think through this." (Year Three)

When she continued, it was clear that Pat still did not focus on the mastery of specific concepts or facts:

From almost everything we do I want them to start to realize that there's a reason. And with the physical sciences we're starting off with the kids don't even know where to begin to ask questions. . . . I want them to have experiences here, and at home with their take-home labs, that later on, when they experience them again, other places, they think about some of the concepts behind it. And not

even that they know the exact concepts, but that they know there *is*
one. "Oh yeah, there's a reason why this is a pattern." I like them
while they're here to know what that reason is, but once they leave
me, they probably aren't going to remember, so I just want them to
remember that "Oh, yeah, there is a reason for this. There is some
sort of thing behind this, there's a theory behind this." (Year Three)

Pat noted that students often came into biology classes with questions.
She was not as intrigued by those questions as she once had been, and
actually found some of the questions difficult. "With animals and life science, they have lots of questions. There's all sorts of weird things they ask."
I had asked Pat if she worried that her students might come up with
some misconceptions because of her physical science class, and she said
that they more than likely would, but that would not matter. What was
important was that they would later be interested when they came across
the idea in another setting. I then wondered:

Deb: Do you think you'd have that same orientation if you were in high
   school?
Pat: (Sigh)—You mean [with] that "Prepare them for college sort of
   thing?" I probably wouldn't be allowed to have that much [free-
   dom]; however, it depends who I was teaching. . . . If I had a test to
   teach for, I would teach for it. And if it was important that my
   students pass it, I would teach for it. But that's my philosophy of
   teaching. My philosophy of teaching is that while they're with me,
   they have fun and they think "Wow," or "Oh neat." . . . My philosophy is to give them something to think about. (Year Three)

Pat described one student who was probably failing and said that failing her course was very unlikely, that very few students who attended class
failed. I asked why, and she replied that they all knew what would be covered on tests.

Pat: They know *exactly* what's going to be on the test, 'cause I want
   them to know that stuff so they know it's going to be on the test.
Deb: I want to ask about the tests. What kind of tests are you giving
   them?
Pat: Well, I'm doing several different kinds. (she laughs) We had a test
   this time, it was a partner test. And it was all based on reading an
   article. . . . The first part was written and each partner had to write
   [something]. The second part, the second day, was a lab on how
   well they could figure out how to do this lab with these balloons

and clay. It was all modeling rockets and satellites. So that's one of them.

I'm doing tests that have a hands-on assessment where they have to come back [to the lab tables] and they have to do something. . . . I also do tests where I just redo a demo or two demos that I've already done, and we've already discussed. And then they are to write and discuss again.

Almost all my tests are essay. And then a few, every once in a while some fill in the blank things, for just vocabulary and that sort of thing. But I've never had a test that doesn't consist mostly of essay. (Year Three)

SUMMARY

Even though Pat was conscious as a junior of the need to take charge of her own learning, it took quite a while for her to develop confidence and strategies for working through her confusions. As a junior and senior she did not describe many explicit strategies she used to monitor her developing understanding and, in fact, thought that she learned some things without being conscious of the learning. She also had doubted the value of what she knew until her senior year, when she realized that she had studied the same material in several classes and that it was the important material. Her classwork with Fred, after student teaching, contributed to her ability to describe specific strategies for learning and to her confidence.

Pat valued biology because it could provide mechanisms or reasons that explained observed phenomena. After her student teaching she described biology as a field of study that was fascinating and engaging and that could provide learners with the enjoyment of interesting things to think about. She did not emphasize specific biology content that was essential to teach, but was more interested that her students realize there were explanations.

Pat recognized early that learning could be serendipitous and that people learned differently, and after completing student teaching seemed comfortable with the uncertainty in teaching. These beliefs seemed to contribute to her use of many kinds of assignments and assessments in her own teaching. As a middle school teacher she had little pressure to teach specific content, and the freedom to explore content and methods. She avoided lecturing and experimented with projects. She tried to help her students learn to gather and evaluate information and make claims.

As a junior Pat saw labs as important because learners could engage with real phenomena and ask questions. She did not stress using labs to teach experimental method or scientific thinking and, in fact, never felt that there was any unique scientific method. She thought that critical thinking and a healthy skepticism were the central elements. Pat was critical of standard laboratory exercises because she had only followed procedures and had not developed any personal meaning for the work.

Pat's teaching assignments changed over the 3 years, but her general approach remained. She had recognized early that students vary in the ways they approach learning and get engaged, so she planned for variety in her classroom activities. In her teaching, she worked to make clear to students that scientific theories helped to explain patterns in the everyday world by exploring the mechanisms producing these patterns. She also, though, hoped that students would learn that people developed these theories and that they would have the confidence to develop their own. Her concern that students develop a sense of efficacy as learners reflected her interpretation of her early learning experiences when she failed to question. For Pat, a personal connection to the content was crucial for further understanding—whether it was the interest of a teacher or the realization that the scientists doing the work were nearby or seeing the material in the popular press. She planned her teaching to foster these personal connections. In an earlier article about Pat (Trumbull, 1996), I speculated that Pat's awareness of the serendipity of learning was central to her growth as a teacher. Because she recognized that there were no certain methods that could engender learning, she was not searching for that one right way, but looked for a range of good ways to stimulate thinking and learning. She did not identify specific content that was essential to teach, but felt that students should be able to use the content they studied. She did not speak of learning separate from content. Her emphasis on asking questions reflects her understanding that biological knowledge is continually changing.

CHAPTER 4

Sylvie Andrews

I chose the pseudonym Sylvie after the Schubert song "Wer ist Sylvie" (Who is Sylvie?) because it took me a while to understand her: she was uncertain and tentative initially. She spoke little in classes and initially was less forthcoming in interviews than were others. Our interviews improved when I realized she talked more in informal situations. When I visited her, she often drove me around and we went out to eat at each visit. I could follow up on our chatting when we sat down for the formal interviews. I used the name Andrews because of Julie Andrews, since it was a musical connection that produced her first name.

I taught the pre-student teaching seminar Sylvie took, but did not supervise her student teaching. I interviewed Sylvie the first time when she was a senior. She was the only one of the six new teachers who did not attend the Shoals Adaptions class. Sylvie did her student teaching in a rural high school with a cooperating teacher who was an accomplished traditional teacher.

The year after graduating, Sylvie did not find a teaching job, so she worked at an environmental agency in a large metropolitan area. She found a teaching position in an affluent suburb the next year. Sylvie taught high school biology and chemistry for 2 years at this large suburban high school. There were no mandated end-of-year examinations in this state, although there were biology and chemistry curricula that were shared among all the teachers. Sylvie had her own biology classroom the first year, with an attached preparation area. She moved to another room for chemistry classes. The second year, she did not have her own classroom and could not reach a prep area without passing through someone else's class.

Sylvie moved, and began her third year of teaching in a troubled urban high school. The teaching was extremely difficult and after other teachers resigned, Sylvie did too. She found a new position in the middle of the year in a smaller middle school some distance from the urban center. There she taught middle school science, the curriculum for which included a mix of the sciences. She was the third teacher in that class and inherited a classroom with decorations, displays, and animals left from the first teacher.

She started work in February, and when I visited her, she had been in the school about 3 months.

LEARNING

Sylvie did not think of herself as a Cornell student. Frustratingly, I did not explore why she felt uninvolved in typical courses.

Syl: I don't think I'm a very good learner a lot of the time. I don't think I really throw myself into anything. . . . I think that if it comes up outside of the class, then I'm more interested in it. I guess I'm pretty typical of an average student. Not that interested unless it's presented in a different type of way. Like auto-tutorial is a lot better than lecture. . . . I don't know how I got to Cornell, 'cause I'm not a good, not an ideal student.

Deb: What would be ideal?

Syl: I see it in other people in the program. Like Elaine or Joan. They just totally are into their classes . . . just find interest in every class and really throw themselves into what they're doing and—

Sylvie liked studying with others for "just the comfort of having someone with you." She described her study strategy as "the typical read, go over my notes and if I have any problems ask my friend I'm studying with." Sylvie did not say that she discussed the content or her interpretations with others, and the detail she provided suggests she relied heavily on memorization.

Sylvie felt that in high school biology classes teachers simplified the content: "They're not telling you the whole story. Because there is so much to each thing, they simplify a lot." She had problems and thought other students did also:

I think I look into things too much and make things more complicated. . . . I know that a lot of times high school students will [say], "Just tell me what I need to know, . . . don't make it more complicated." And teachers . . . try to simplify everything. And I'm always trying to understand things deeper and I think that for some reason that gets me in trouble and I don't think it should. (Senior)

To determine what Sylvie considered important for a deeper understanding, I asked her for an example of something she was studying that she didn't quite understand. She gave a very general description of countercurrent mechanisms, which seems to match the general overview she had criticized. In the interview, I did not help Sylvie clarify her thinking. I could at least have asked her to clarify some of her terms or give more specific examples. At the time, I was trying to be supportive and encouraging.

Syl: It's in a lot of places and there's things going in the opposite direction to increase the concentration. The concentration gradients are going the opposite directions. I think that's it. So that there will be more of a concentration gradient across the different [areas]. But I don't understand how it's working, as you can tell from the entire explanation.
Deb: No, that sounds pretty reasonable.
Syl: But I don't understand why that's happening. (Senior)

I asked her how she knew when she understood something. Her response did not reveal any strategies to monitor her work, although she was looking for a molecular explanation of mechanisms. Her comment may indicate a realization that much of biology is incompletely understood, but I failed to follow up.

Syl: (Long pause) I just have a feeling. And a lot of times I don't think I understand. (laughs apologetically)
Deb: Like with countercurrent mechanisms? What.
Syl: I think if I understand every single aspect, . . . if I can relate what I've learned from physics and chemistry to that, then I'll know that I understand it. But it's so hard, 'cause in biology they might just not be able to explain everything about it. (Senior)

I asked her what would be different if she really understood countercurrent mechanisms. "I think I'd just feel confident when I was explaining it to someone. But my explanation probably wouldn't be any different." (Senior)
Sylvie's description of herself as learner provides a metaphor for what she seemed like at that time, as did her concern about giving the right answer to my probe.

Syl: I find that I don't think I'm a true scientist sometimes, I . . . can't see certain things that other people seem to see.
Deb: Like?—Can you give me an example?
Syl: Yeah, I'm thinking. I don't know if this is the right idea. We were looking at fossils in botany and I didn't see them. And so there's all these kids saying, "Wow, that's really cool." . . . And I couldn't even see anything. (Senior)

Sylvie contrasted memorization to understanding, and clearly felt memorization was important in learning. It is not clear just what she meant by understanding or by "scientific." She explained:

> I didn't learn history the way I think it should be taught. And maybe it would be scientific . . . to me history was just memorization and so it's not . . . I mean, they're both memorizing, but there was no understanding in history. And I think maybe if it was taught in a different way it'd be similar to biology. (Senior)

Sylvie had done some tutoring and remembered feeling bad for some students because "they studied and they came in to me for help, but they just could not take the professor's tests, did really bad." She did not analyze why they had problems on the tests. I asked her about gauging students' understanding, and she used invented dialogue that captured well common student behaviors, but lacked speculation about reasons or strategies she could use.

Deb: When you're working with someone, how can you tell if they understand something?
Syl: What I'll usually do is I'll ask them questions and then see if they— But it's so hard. I still don't know. Because when I say, "Do you guys understand this, 'cause you're not looking like you understand this?" And they say, "Yeah, yeah, we understand it." I guess I'll quit the "Do you understand?" question. (laughs) No one seems to answer truthfully. (Senior)

I repeated this question in the interview after Sylvie's student teaching, and her response was nearly identical. She did add that responses on a "certain assignment" could provide information but, "I don't know if they really do [understand]."

In her MAT interview, Sylvie reported using concept mapping to help her clarify lecture material. Although concept mapping helped Sylvie determine that these lectures were poorly organized, she did not say using this strategy increased her understanding. She criticized some Cornell teachers, noting that their poor teaching ensured success for only a few students.

Deb: How do you describe yourself as a learner now?
Syl: Well, I guess I blame the teacher more than I used to. [For example], there is this male [guest lecturer] in physiology class. The head teacher is really good; he taught the first week. Everything was very

clear and it made sense and we were looking at the overall picture, but now this guy is teaching us. . . . He seems very nice but it seems like his lectures are all over the place.

Last night I was trying to work a problem set of his and I was looking at the lecture notes, and finally I said, "OK, I'm going to concept map this." . . . So I did and it was just his lectures were horrible. And now it's more like I blame the professors of science because they really make things a lot more difficult than they need to make them. Only a few people can make it out. (MAT)

Sylvie's description of herself at this time suggests that she was trying not to rely on memorization to pass tests. I wonder now if her anxiety was due to her shaky grasp of the material or to a fear that the test would be poorly written. She said:

Just making the concept map last night . . . I was thinking, "Oh, but I'm not going to go through what I normally go through with these classes where I just try to memorize bits and pieces and hope something that I memorized shows up on a multiple choice test." You know, for science classes I did that, but there's a desperate feeling. More looking at trying to make the lecture clear, the overall picture. Even though I could do this and my doing that last night did not help me on a problem set, and it might not help me on the test, so, who knows? (MAT)

BIOLOGY

As a senior, Sylvie felt that biology was inherently interesting because "that's your body, your health," but noted that students often needed a teacher to point out the relevance. She said that biology was connected to other sciences, but that she had realized this only in her college studies. Sylvie thought that biology was appealing because high school students could perform better in biology than in other sciences. They could "get by, by memorizing in high school biology. So they might have more confidence about that than physics or chemistry, so they might not be as turned off."

I think many of Sylvie's remarks reflected an unarticulated criticism of biology teaching that she had experienced. I label her critique unarticulated because when I asked her for details, she did not supply any, seemed to retreat from a solid critique, and presented no alternative.

Deb: What do think, and you've kind of talked about this, the purpose of biology courses should be in high school?

Syl: To stimulate interest. (firmly) They definitely should. I'm sorry but . . . I don't think you're going to have all this great body of knowledge from high school biology. You will learn basic things, but it really should be to stimulate interest. It's the first science class you have, and it shouldn't scare people away from science. And I think that it does.

Deb: Have you seen anything about the way that intro bio is taught in high school that makes it harder for students?

Syl: It's just more material, perhaps. I don't know. I can't see what makes it hard right now. I haven't seen enough. (Senior)

Attention from a teacher had been important to Sylvie's interest in science, although at other times during our interviews she would aver it was important for students to become independent. In her senior year interview she mentioned the importance of two mentors and faulted other teachers for not offering enough guidance or structure. She had been fascinated by biology lessons from the school nurse in fourth grade, but then lost interest in science. She recalled:

I just remember not liking it [science] after that 'cause it was always physical science. And the teachers were sort of like, "Go off and do your own projects," but they never guided us. . . . I never really understood what was going on.

And then in eighth grade . . . I think my teacher really liked me and she asked me to be in the special group and we went off on nature walks. And that's when I was reintroduced. Then I really liked it for the rest of high school. . . . I really liked biology. (Senior)

In the interview after her student teaching I tried to elicit her evaluations. She did not like it that her cooperating teacher had not slowed down progress through the curriculum, even though many students did very poorly on the examination. I think she referred to the chemistry content as an "accounting skill" because it would be used in later units.

Deb: Does your cooperating teacher kind of go through the Regents curriculum pretty tightly?

Syl: Yeah. . . . It's kind of bad like because you have biochemistry to begin with, and [students] didn't know what the heck was going on. And then I said something like, "OK, we'll do a review or something and how it was related to biochemistry." This kid was like, "Oh, so if we didn't learn it the first time." And I said, "Well, now you'll learn it 'cause it's kind of an accounting skill." (MAT)

Asked about any negative things in her student teaching, Sylvie referred to her biology knowledge and her ability to command respect in the classroom, thus linking them implicitly. She did not want to be the kind of teacher seen as the font of all knowledge, but had no articulated alternative. She had tried strategies to deal with areas about which she did not know, but did not seem pleased with any of them, perhaps because they were not used by other teachers in the school.

Syl: I don't know if this is negative, but subject matter wise, just . . . no, that's not all that negative. I guess, like all the questions I didn't know the answers to. . . . But it was more the beginning, not commanding respect, and that type of thing.

Deb: And you eventually learned to do that?

Syl: I don't know if I learned to do it as much as it just came with time. . . . Whenever I didn't know, I just said, "I don't know." And then I would go check on what the answers were, and sometimes I would get back to them and other times I wouldn't. Another thing is I would kind of stop and think about the answer to a question for a while, and I would start out with, "Well, I'm not that sure but. . . ." And I think that . . . that was a bad thing for them, but I'm not so sure that was such a bad thing. . . . I don't want a classroom to be like, "Da da da da, da da da da (hums) . . . and here's the answer." Which I think that they're kind of used to. (MAT)

LABORATORY INSTRUCTION

When she was a senior, Sylvie viewed lab activities as a way to help students better learn the content of the class. Lab "should always be really related to what you're doing in class [lecture]. So it has a purpose, so people know you're doing it for a reason."

From her observations in a local high school, she also had seen that lab activities afforded teachers a chance to work with individual students, and reported being "shocked at the answers" some students gave to the teacher's questions. In her senior year she took a field ecology class that had labs without fully scripted procedures. Students began with a central question about which they had to collect and analyze data, and Sylvie reported these as her first labs that emphasized learning science methods.

Deb: Some people have said that science labs are really important because they teach kids scientific method. What do you think about that?

Syl: I don't think I learned how to really deal with that until this semester. I took a field ecology class where we spent 5 hours every Friday collecting a lot of data. And then it wasn't until way into the semester that I realized there's so many ways of looking at the data. And I don't think I ever got that from high school. I mean, it may be good if it did, but I don't see it doing that now. (Senior)

Sylvie did not describe doing many lab activities during her student teaching. She had talked to another teacher about possible ideas for innovative labs. He pointed out how hard it was to change students' expectations, and Sylvie seemed to have abandoned the efforts to develop her own labs. She recalled:

> I was talking to Elaine's cooperating teacher. . . . I was asking him for lab ideas and he said, "You can't expect them to come up with their own hypotheses. That's just really too much to ask for, when they're used to cookbook labs. It's not really fair." And I'm not going to go around blaming the kids for that. You know these kids have no creativity, I mean I think you can work towards that, but I don't want to expect too much of that. (MAT)

PRACTICE AS A NEW TEACHER—YEAR ONE

I asked Sylvie if she had made any changes to the school's biology curriculum. She mentioned using major themes to focus her curriculum but was not clear about how she used them to make decisions. She was struggling to present an overall framework without burdening students with too much vocabulary and detail.

Deb: How'd you decide what to not cover?

Syl: It's hard. For example, for anything where there's a lot of vocabulary. And they even complain that I use words that are too fancy. But I've cut it down a lot . . . like respiration and photosynthesis. Like knowing all the steps—forget it!

Deb: So you [give] kind of the overview?

Syl: Yeah. (Year One)

Sylvie described some biology content as boring but necessary, related to her belief that there were certain fundamental or basic ideas that were

necessary for grasping the material in other units. It appeared Sylvie felt
that this material had to be memorized.

Deb: Do you have anything more to say about units that are boring? I
think it was in connection with some of the biology units that were
more boring than the chemistry?
Syl: Yeah . . . it seems like you just have to get through it, you know?
Deb: Just because it's required and they need it?
Syl: As one of my friends put it, we were arguing about education, and
he was talking about memorizing stuff. And I'm like, "No, No," and
he's like, "Listen, you can't manipulate variables if you have no
variables to manipulate." So there's a certain amount of basic
knowledge that people have to have. . . . So you just have to plow
through it. And I don't think it's going to be exciting. (Year One)

Sylvie's belief in the cumulative nature of biology, in which basic
knowledge was a necessary first step, was also apparent in her analysis
of difficulties faced by underachievers. "I think that's the thing with real
underachievers, is they come in and out. When they decide to do well
they don't have the material that they need . . . so they get discouraged
again." (Year One)

Sylvie used the labs that the other teachers in the school used. These
lab activities required students to work in groups and to submit one lab
report per group. Although this arrangement could have developed from
an effort to innovate and support cooperative learning, Sylvie felt it was
done for expedience,

because the teachers are fed up with doing a lot of work. They used
to all get merit pay and that's been cut, so they said, "Okay, we're
just going to do group labs."

Sylvie modified the procedure because she had observed that these
group reports allowed some students to avoid work. She required each
person in the group to complete and turn in a report, then would grade
only one report from the group. She felt that even if some of the lab report
was "busy work, and it might be a little bit, but at least if they're *all* writing, they're somehow at least all somewhat involved." She clearly did not
see the work students did on the lab reports as a cooperative endeavor that
would involve everyone and increase everyone's learning.

Sylvie relied on multiple choice tests. She thought her students needed
to be accountable and to learn responsibility. Her concern with individual
effort was also apparent in discussing tests:

The test is, in my opinion, it's unfortunate, but it's the one situation where these kids aren't cheating from each other. The individual counts at that point. (Year one)

PRACTICE AS A NEW TEACHER—YEAR TWO

We chatted at dinner the night before I came to Sylvie's school. Some of the things we talked about at dinner included balancing discipline with affirmation. She worried that she was too critical of students. She had begun to adapt district objectives and give them to students to orient their work.

Deb: What's it like being a teacher this second year?
Syl: Uhm, good. (said tentatively, and we laugh). Up and down. It's easier, but I still get discouraged. I went through long blocks of time getting really discouraged by the motivation of the kids.

In her second year Sylvie had students prepare and present two group reports, a practice she had begun the year before because other teachers did it. When I visited her in the second year, student groups were presenting reports on invertebrate groups. Sylvie had not remembered covering the invertebrate groups in high school, but thought it was a good idea for students to be exposed to the material and to prepare the reports. The Mollusk group brought in clams and opened them in class, a process that was time-consuming and tried my patience as an observer. I asked Sylvie what she thought about it. "That was a little crazy. But it seemed like everyone was somehow focused on it, so it didn't really bother me."

Her own subject matter knowledge remained an issue. She thought she should "keep a notebook of questions they ask, which I haven't done. Because I know I won't be able to answer all the questions, but I know there's a lot I can answer."

Sylvie had no state curriculum that students had to learn, so as a teacher, "here, you're not accountable for anything. So if your kids are failing you can always do extra credit." Sylvie did not express a strong commitment to covering any particular content. "I do not have an opinion, necessarily, on which topics should be taught. My opinion would be nothing revolutionary. I probably would agree with what's being taught, and what's required of us."

In her first year, Sylvie had used tests with multiple choice questions and she continued to use them in her second year, because of the time it took her to correct tests. In her second year she tried varying her tests, assignments, and quizzes somewhat, according to the content being tested.

Sylvie distinguished between material to which learners should be exposed
and material that was more important to understand, and devised ways
to avoid lecturing on the more straightforward material, in the process
creating another way to teach responsibility.

Syl: So much biology it seems is memorizing, so if [the material] is more
on that end, "Expose yourself to this," then, I put the responsibility
on them. But if it's hard to understand, then I take the time to
discuss it.

Deb: What are your quizzes and tests like?

Syl: They vary depending on the subject matter. For example, for
genetics it wasn't an open-note test, it was traditional, because I
didn't think notes would help them. . . . We've had open-note
quizzes for a while now; they should know that if they don't
understand it, this [review sheet] isn't going to help! [This year I'm
using] more open-note quizzes and tests because it puts the responsibility on them. And I don't have to lecture on it. They can read it
on their own in the book.

Deb: Oh, so when you say open-note, those are the notes that come from
their reading of the book.

Syl: Yes. And that way it just makes them more accountable. . . .

Deb: I think you said last night, that you were beginning to use some
objectives for the different units?

Syl: Right. And for the last couple of quizzes I would give them the quiz
questions beforehand (rising inflection). So all they had to do was
answer them and bring those. . . . The point is that it rewards hard
work and there's really no excuse not to do well. (Year Two)

Sylvie made some changes in testing. "When I gave them the test questions beforehand, [they were] short essays [with] paragraph answers."
However, she continued to rely primarily on multiple choice questions for
her tests, and worried about the content validity of her questions.

Deb: Are you getting good at writing multiple choice questions?

Syl: No. I usually get them from a test bank, but now I'm trying to get
away from it. Because I usually thought it saved time? But now I
realize it doesn't because you spend so much time looking for good
questions that it's probably easier just to write a test. And in the end
I think writing the tests is more fair (rising inflection).

Deb: Because?

Syl: Oh, just so you can have the questions be just a little bit more direct.
And the kids see, "Oh, we did this. It doesn't look totally foreign."
(Year Two)

In her second year, Sylvie gathered data about her students that helped her interpret their actions. For example, she realized that students' scores on the SAT exams were not exceptional. "Everyone always says the students here are the cream of the crop, it really isn't so. . . . School is not where their priorities are, they're typical teenagers." Once she realized this she could see that some of her students' problems were not due to poor teaching on her part.

PRACTICE AS A NEW TEACHER—YEAR THREE

After moving to the middle school in midyear, Sylvie taught seventh-grade science classes. After reviewing our earlier interviews, I had decided to provide Sylvie more comments about the things I thought she was doing well because I felt as though the reassurance would be important to her. The middle school teaching seemed to be benefiting her. Sylvie had a busy schedule for the classes when I observed. Students discussed water quality and soil issues and tended their garden plots.

Deb: Another thing I noticed that you're doing so well, is—you say your first-period students are your guinea pigs—you built upon each period, you got a little bit more sophistication [with each period]. I mean, you're really learning.
Syl: I don't mind teaching the same course all day. I do not get bored. . . . I get tired! But I can't say I'm bored, with the lesson. (Year Three)

When I observed her in the third year, Sylvie wrote out plans on the board and had students copy expectations into planning books. She appeared well-organized and decisive. This was a strength I wanted to point out to her. Although she had not developed the planning book policy, she was able to evaluate its effect on the students.

Deb: That was really a good use of the blackboard. I mean they really pay attention to what's listed and what they need to do for their planning books.
Syl: Yeah. Now that's another good idea to do that [use planning books] to avoid the inevitable question of "What are we going to do today?" Because that happens in every class. Even when I was teaching chemistry. I don't know why, maybe to be prepared, or something like that. (Year Three)

Sylvie appeared to have developed a new understanding of the role of the teacher and the ways that she could fulfill that role. The elaboration she gave in the following answer reflected her thinking. She articulated a view of knowledge and understanding as less certain and more serendipitous, and was using the interview to speculate more explicitly. As a teacher she continued to use interest and engagement to evaluate student performance, but trusted herself enough to rely on more than test grades to evaluate learners. I asked her if she was different.

Syl: Definitely, because I try to realize what's important to have control over, and then sort of relinquish control over other things.
Deb: Like?
Syl: Well, like I don't try to fill up every minute of the class. I realize it's important to sort of have a little bit of time, not to feel totally stressed out if kids have to deal with their own little issues at the beginning of class.
     Grading classes is different; it's much cloudier now. I think I try to play favorites a little bit more now. Before I used to be very by the book, by the numbers.
Deb: How do you then deal with the fear that you might be unfair?
Syl: Well, I still try to be fair, but I guess my definition of fair has changed (slight laugh). Like if someone—what am I trying to say? Like I will give more breaks to kids now, but it is a break, and if the kid has not shown himself deserving of the break, I will not give it to them. Like I was saying, I'm probably a lot more cloudy in my grading. (Year Three)

Sylvie was a bit frustrated that there were no curriculum guidelines for this middle school class to indicate what students had studied previously because, "I don't want them to say, 'Well, we already did this last year. We've seen this video before.'" For curriculum guidelines Sylvie would have liked "just something that says 'cover volcanoes.' Not what you had to do, but just that sort of thing." In her third year she was still not driven by concerns about what students had to know, but said she was interested in having them learn about things such as protecting the environment. At one point she said, with a laugh, "I mean I kind of have in the back of my mind that they really, really are going to forget everything." However, after some time she revealed her overall aim.

Deb: So how about you, Sylvie Andrews, cool teacher? If you could talk to these kids 2 years later, what would you want them to say they remember? They've gotten out of seventh grade?
Syl: —I guess I'd think that if they were walking along on a hike, I'd just hope . . . I just did all this geology stuff, I really have this wonder

about, not only the animals and plants around me, but, for example, sometimes when I drive I'll notice one of those anticlines and synclines, and wonder "How did that get there?" And notice, have them think more about that. "There were volcanoes right in this area, there was igneous rock." So they should think about this when they see a rock. . . . I think that really, everything is very complex, when you think about it. Everything they see around them, when you start thinking about where it came from, and what it means. (Year Three)

Sylvie said she had good days, but not every day was fun. She said that in 5 years she did not want to be considered "really cool or . . . really hard, demanding. But just a good teacher." She thought it would be great if students learned they could not misbehave in her class because misbehavior created more work for her, but it was "still important to me that kids don't feel intimidated." She limited her goals to being a good teacher because "my sanity and personal life are important."

Deb: There seems to be a negative image behind what you're saying. You say you want to be just a good teacher, you don't want to sacrifice everything.
Syl: Yeah.
Deb: What would a teacher who sacrificed social life or personal life and sanity what would—
Syl: I just think they become bitter. I don't think they can last that long. I think that happened to A. [at former high school] She did sacrifice an awful lot for that school and department. And she just about burned out. . . . Whereas other teachers in that department were . . . probably just as good teachers, but they weren't going on with the newest reforms. They could use older—they weren't always doing the workshops and taking all the classes. So they were just happier, more content people. (Year Three)

I tried to determine whether or not she had felt these misgivings when she was at the school, but had not voiced them to me. Her answer revealed an increased confidence in herself as a teacher and a willingness to evaluate carefully any suggestions for teaching. As I asked this question, Sylvie interjected assent several times. I have put these in uppercase to illustrate the rapid flow of the talk and her involvement.

Deb: I just wondered if maybe at the time you were feeling guilty because YEAH you weren't ready for that [pressure] UH HUH and you were being pushed and pulled and it's hard as a new teacher to say, "No, I don't want to."

Syl: Yeah. Not guilty, but influenced. But now I guess I can say, "Well that's a good idea, I might try that." I probably would, I'd probably try anything new. Not that I would keep doing it . . . if it didn't work.

Sylvie proceeded to comment about what she had not liked about her former school. She felt that they did not have clear goals for what would be taught in each unit, and that teachers curved grades by adding points, to ensure the students gained high grades. She said teachers justified the curving by saying, "Well, hopefully they picked up something."

Sylvie then used her concern over clear goals and standards for passing exams by analyzing the curving that was practiced at Cornell. Note that Sylvie now can describe herself as being in a cloud during her time at Cornell, which she felt was a result of specific aspects of teaching.

Syl: I don't believe in curving. At Cornell. I mean, I really think they should put some thought into . . . what they want to teach us, what they can expect to teach us, teach us that, and test us on that. Instead, what they seemed to do is just dump so much information, and test on so much information, and see what happens. (She laughs angrily)

Deb: That's definitely what they do.

Syl: Not only that, but I just really do not think you learn as much if you don't really know what you are supposed to be learning. I really felt that a lot in my classes, like I was kind of going through this cloud. (Year Three)

SUMMARY

In her senior interview, Sylvie focused on affective factors associated with learning, such as feeling confident, being motivated, or having support from peers. She did not describe any strategies she used to monitor her developing understanding nor did she offer much detail about how one could determine someone else's understanding, even after student teaching. Sylvie did not think she was a good Cornell student and felt typical course structures inhibited her learning, but offered no detail. Although she contrasted memorization to understanding, it was unclear what she meant by understanding. She did not refer to being able to solve a problem or predict a possible physiological effect as evidence of understanding, even though we had talked about physiology. She consistently manifested a belief that memorization was required for most biology learning, with some modifications to this view in her third year of teaching. In her MAT interview she mentioned using only one technique, concept mapping, to help her make sense of material and gain an overview, but she gave no evidence the technique worked for her. In this interview she blamed instructors for not making things clear.

Sylvie initially thought that biology should be interesting to everyone because it involved one's body, but knew that it was not, although she was uncertain why. Her strongest opinion about high school biology was that it should stimulate student interest in further study. Sylvie rarely had much to say about laboratory teaching, appearing to view it primarily as a means to help students understand content.

Partly because she relied on memorization for much of her learning, and used her performance on examinations to gauge her understanding, she was uncertain through much of her Cornell career. In her first teaching job, she felt pressure to adopt new techniques and methods, but did not have the confidence to evaluate these. She seemed to assume that difficulties students had were her fault, and the reputation promulgated by the school culture made it harder for her to realize that many of her students just did not work hard. She had tried to decrease the vocabulary covered in the class, but articulated no strong vision for her teaching until the third year.

As a new teacher Sylvie worried about her subject matter knowledge and how to deal with student questions she could not answer. In her second year of teaching she distinguished content that students could learn on their own from content that she had to help them grasp. In her second year she also came to realize that her students were not gifted, and this finding enabled her to take less responsibility for their poor performances.

Except for the last year, Sylvie's opinions and ideas either seemed based on what others had told her or were offered with little elaboration or supporting evidence. Sylvie's changes over time reflect an increase in confidence and trust in her opinions. I think she had many insights but did not develop them. Perhaps some of the problems I had in interviewing her stemmed from her assumption that her insights were not valid or that she should have had strong opinions about aspects of teaching. She had acknowledged that some things were hard to do, but perhaps thought the difficulties were personal failures, rather than endemic to teaching. When Sylvie read the full case study of her, she wrote me: "Everything looks fine to me. Very interesting. Actually, I wasn't as clueless as I thought."

In year three, in middle school, Sylvie gave up feeling that she had to control every aspect of class and began to trust her own interpretations of students. She was also much more explicit in her critique of her former high school and her classes at Cornell. Traces of these critiques are apparent in earlier interviews, but she did not develop them. In her third year Sylvie was willing to try a new technique to test it out, but said she would continue to use it only if it worked. She aimed to help her students see their worlds differently and understand some of the processes underlying observed phenomena. To the end, she was not committed to teaching certain content and welcomed curriculum guides.

CHAPTER 5

Elaine Spring

Elaine was an ideal interviewee—eager, articulate, thoughtful. Her ideas tumbled out in sentences laced with qualifying phrases, details, and tangents. I edited out the qualifiers and at least some of the tangents to make her quotes easier to read, but kept a few almost intact when it was important to show her thinking.

I taught the pre-student teaching seminar but did not supervise Elaine's student teaching. Elaine did her student teaching with Sam, with whom Fred had worked, and taught high school biology and a middle school unit.

Like Sylvie, Elaine did not find a teaching position after completing her degree, so worked for an outdoor education program for a year. Elaine then found a teaching position in an eastern state, in an area that was experiencing population growth and changing to a suburb. Elaine taught high school biology. The state in which she taught had no mandated curriculum or end-of-year examination.

In her first year, she taught classes with both college-preparatory and non-college-preparatory (general) students. The general biology students were very difficult for her to deal with. In her second year, a more experienced teacher switched classes so that Elaine had only college-prep biology classes. During her first 2 years Elaine had no classroom of her own, but moved from room to room, carrying supplies for any activities on a cart. Elaine had only a small desk in a room shared by all the science teachers.

In her third year of teaching Elaine was placed in one of the trailers that provided supplemental space for the school, and quickly converted that into her own place, with bulletin boards, animals, plants, displays of student work, and other materials. Elaine was again teaching the college-preparatory and non-college-prep students, but was much better than in her first year at working productively with the non-college-prep students.

Although I always felt comfortable interviewing Elaine, I think we began to relate more easily during her second year of teaching. Over dinner the night before I came to class, she told me that she inadvertently had made a pupil cry in class and felt bad. I had once made Elaine cry in class, and I think she realized how it was possible to do this.

I named Elaine through one of those tricks of memory. She had told me, in passing, that one of her students had said that she reminded him of the character named Elaine on the television show "Seinfeld" and she thought that was just outrageous because she was not at all like that character. I agreed, but for some reason forgot that conversation when I chose the name Elaine. I picked the surname Spring because it fit her personality.

LEARNING

As a senior, Elaine did not think that memorization or learning algorithms was good learning. She thought students should learn concepts, not details, but added, "I'm not sure what I mean by conceptual." She felt teachers could facilitate conceptual learning by using good analogies "or something that they [students] could picture."

Elaine was pleased that she was able to apply what she had studied on a recent test. Her description of studying revealed several of her beliefs about learning: that it requires time, active questioning, feedback to check one's interpretation, and attention to all the relevant material, and that learning results in an understanding of mechanisms that will enable one to figure things out. Her desire to learn was strong enough for her to overcome her anxiety about asking the professor questions. She stated:

> The last [test], I was worried 'cause . . . for about 3 or 4 weeks I didn't do anything, except go to lecture. . . . And I pretty much thought I knew what was going on. But it piles up. There was, like, 14 lectures. And all the reading and stuff. So maybe 2 weeks before, I started doing the reading. And there was just a lot of reading. And I had all these things to do before. But I knew I had to do this test. And I knew it was going to be a multiple choice. So I was kind of nuts. But I ended up doing OK.
>
> And I just kind of went through—I had [prepared lecture notes]. And I had my notes, and I went through those. And I went to a review session with the professor, and I asked some questions, even though I felt like, "God, this'll be really dumb." And one of the ones that was really dumb . . . [I found that] I didn't understand the concept at all. Sometimes I do learn things [wrong]. Just the way it works. . . .
>
> The way I went about it was, "I want to understand the concepts." And the way I went about the test was, I kind of understood the basic concepts, and I understood some of the terms, not all of them. But I went over this practice test, and I realized . . . I don't

even know the things in this question. I didn't know . . . the words? But I used whatever we had—and I figured it out. . . . It makes you feel good that you really understood it. (Senior)

As a senior, Elaine had done some tutoring and found that "when I was trying to do a lesson was when I learned the most about how it worked." When tutoring, Elaine tried to grasp how the learner was thinking before she tried to teach, and admitted that she was not always comfortable with her tutoring, but thought that "when I'm teaching I'll probably really get to . . . feeling even more comfortable."

Elaine felt evaluating someone's understanding could be difficult because people would sometimes pretend to understand. She felt, therefore, that a teacher had to gather evidence from other sources. She explained:

Well, on surface things a lot of times you can see it. But sometimes people will pretend they understand when they actually don't . . . I think a lot of times those kids will initiate a question that kind of makes you see whether or not they're understanding it or something. "So, is it like this?" . . . Or other times I'll ask a question that I think will see if they understand. (Senior)

Elaine said that when she understood something she could visualize "how it works." When she studied, "Sometimes I'll ask a question and then I'll realize that I don't understand it at all! And then I'll go back. And I kind of feel like I have to understand it before I can go on."

Elaine clearly had strategies to monitor her learning. Learning biology changed her way of seeing the world, although her self-doubt appeared in the midst of detail:

And then sometimes I sort of do other things, too. If I can kind of relate it to something else . . . I don't know if it's like understanding it as well as I could, but I'll be walking around, and things just come and jump out at me? . . . like I'll be going out and saying things like, "What's happening to your food?" (Laughs). (Senior)

After her student teaching, Elaine reflected on her students' learning and some confusions that surprised her, which caused her to question her earlier distinction between concepts and terms:

I don't think the kids really got a grasp of the concepts of [protein synthesis], even things I never thought would be a big deal. I . . . had to really emphasize what chromosomes were, what DNA was.

And they were so confused about how DNA and genes and chromosomes are related. . . . In a way, it seems like it's simple facts, but it just turned out to be something that they've just got to think about a lot more. (MAT)

Because Sam, her cooperating teacher, used a range of assessment techniques, Elaine could compare and contrast students' performances on different measures. She noted how hard it was to determine the level of students' understanding:

I think they could probably answer questions really easily on a multiple choice test without really understanding. When we did concept maps and stuff, you'd see that they would connect things in these really weird ways and you'd think like, "Oh, they don't have any idea what a gene is!" because they'd think that a gene is like the stuff that makes up DNA. (MAT)

Elaine learned that students needed specific assignments to ensure they would do the work and learn the needed terms. She explained:

I made up a lot of worksheets for them because they needed something. I felt it was really getting ridiculous, I wished they could just do this. But if they didn't have to write it down a lot of times, they wouldn't really get it. . . . The more I think, I don't think you can learn science without understanding a lot of the words. I mean, you can't read a magazine without knowing the terms. Which is frustrating, but I think it's true. (MAT)

Elaine viewed questioning as important to learning and developed tactics to elicit students' questions. She was especially worried about students who lacked the confidence to ask questions in class, "so I tried to go around more and ask them questions and stuff." She used questions because she found that observing students at work or in discussion did not always help her gauge their understanding. She gathered information to evaluate her work as a teacher. She recalled:

And I have had kids . . . answer questions at the end of class. . . . I asked them once, "What is an adaptation, explain it in terms that someone younger than you could understand and give an example." And I saw then that they all thought it was adjusting to the situation. And I realized that my explanation probably didn't help get rid of the old definition that everyone uses every day. (MAT)

When I asked her about herself as a learner, Elaine first noted that this was a repeat question, and then talked about how her behaviors that related to what she called her own low self-esteem could shape people's perceptions of her:

> Well, one thing I'm working on is the self-esteem. I very much lack confidence in myself and it drives me nuts. I've been catching myself more and more. People will say things like, "Why do you always say, 'This is really stupid, but?'" So I'm really working on trying hard not to always qualify everything I say or—act as though I don't really know something that I'm pretty sure about. I noticed I'd do that when I was teaching. . . . It's an awful role model and it's awful because kids are going to constantly wonder, "Does she really know what she's talking about or is she just full of it?" (MAT)

BIOLOGY

As a senior, Elaine distinguished among different areas in biology when she contrasted her botany class with her physiology class. Botany was "more a memorization class" and physiology emphasized understanding mechanisms, "like all the stages of what's going on and stuff."

Elaine felt that biology was a useful discipline because learners could apply biology content to their lives, but that the terminology was daunting. She reflected:

> I've noticed when I've tried to teach it there's a lot of terms that you have to teach. . . . It seems like the concepts are usually understandable, and you can apply them to things that are going on inside of you. But when you try to get all the terms in, that's sometimes the hard part. (Senior)

Elaine's description of the interconnections in biology helps explain why she found it took so much time to learn:

> I'll get through studying and I'll try to put it all together. And it just seems like so many times it's like the whole body, or something, and you're trying to figure out how it all goes together. (Senior)

Elaine liked exercises that required her to make sense of material by relating it to some fundamental idea to see "the way things all fit together. . . . [For example], you have to discuss how plants probably evolved. Like one week we had to do that in an essay."

Elaine believed that high school biology classes should stress material that would apply to students' lives, which she observed in general classes. She criticized many Regents classes because "I think in school if you're in Regents biology they're trying to give you a background . . . so when you're taking biology when you go to college you'll have a feel for the terms and the concepts and everything."

After her student teaching, Elaine was still concerned about the adequacy of her own knowledge. Her students raised unexpected questions, which provided her an impetus to learn more biology. "So, I didn't expect myself to be an expert about it at all, but I guess if I'm preparing things for the class I want to know about stuff. Taking classes [now] I think about things in a different way."

After student teaching, Elaine believed good teaching should help learners understand mechanisms or reasons for phenomena in the world. She reflected:

> If you think about adaptation, then you get more excited when you see things . . . I mean I do anyway. When you're outside and you see something and you think, "I wonder why that happens?" So I think in a way it's to help keep them interested in it.

LABORATORY INSTRUCTION

As a senior Elaine had seen that labs could help people learn content. She had clear criteria for the content that should be addressed in labs. Elaine mentioned that labs could foster scientific thinking through involving students in designing experiments.

Ela: I think labs should give you something that you can't do in a book, especially in biology, where there are so many things you could do, like a dissection, or using the microscope, or doing an experiment, or something. . . . And just learning how to think scientifically, and stuff like that.

Deb: What does it mean to think scientifically?

Ela: Well, this is the way I think scientifically. You propose a question and think of what you'd expect the answer to be. And then you think of a way to approach that question. I'm always trying to isolate variables and stuff like that. Or think, "Well gee, you can really be looking at this, but maybe something else is going to be influencing it. How are you going to keep it so what you're trying to look at is what you're looking at?" (Senior)

Elaine said that her current field ecology course offered a contrast to the laboratory work in her other courses. She did not emphasize hypothesizing or data analysis. She focused instead on the direct experience, which she preferred. "Last week we did beavers, seeing what trees they chose. You're seeing real trees, and you're going out and you're trying to do it. You had to make measurements and all, but you can see what's going on here."

Elaine had many concerns about laboratory teaching after she completed her student teaching. "I guess I just need more experience. But I just sort of felt like, 'Oh, there has to be something, like more interesting.'" She had difficulty finding labs she liked. Most were "recipe labs. I tried really hard to think of labs that [had students] really thinking about them and asking the questions and developing some strategy to answer the question." Elaine gave an example of an exercise she tried after students failed to make good slides showing mitosis.

Ela: I did this thing where they had to do jumping jacks in the room. . . .
You'd have them start off at all different times, and then you'd
stop them and they had to freeze in whatever position they
were in.
Deb: Like statue.
Ela: But the thing is, I only did that for them. I didn't say, "Now this
is how you're going to relate it." I just did that, and then I said,
"Now you're going to . . . have an onion root tip slide, you're
going to have a microscope. . . . You're going to have to somehow
figure out how you can relate this jumping jack exercise. And
how the frequency that you see something is related to the time.
And then you relate it to how long cells spend in different stages."
Some kids were really pretty frustrated, but they were actually
thinking about it. . . . And some kids were just looking at me
like, "I don't know what we're doing." And I said, "If I were
like this, how many people ended up like this and how many
people ended up like [that]." And they'd say, "Oh, well, let me
see."

Elaine helped the students think through the exercise but concluded with a summary that captured her general ambivalence about trying to develop good lab activities from an interesting idea. "I thought that was neat. But I don't know. I guess it's just really hard because there were all these things I was trying to work on (rising inflection)." Elaine had high goals, but ended her description of labs she had done by saying, "But the labs I actually did, I didn't think were that great."

PRACTICE AS A NEW TEACHER—YEAR ONE

Elaine struggled with teaching specialized vocabulary versus concepts. Her extended quote illustrates one facet of the struggle she faced when given the biology curriculum outline.

> I had a certain amount of freedom, but I'm trying really hard not to be too bogged down in terms. . . . I had the kids talking about what a consumer is, what a producer is, and very comfortably using those terms. Well, I look at the midterm, when I finally got it, a month through school or 2 months through school, it had the words heterotroph and autotroph! I was like, "Oh my God, why don't you just hit me over the head with a 2 by 4! I don't need this. The kids can communicate, and then you tell me I have to use [the terms] heterotroph and autotroph?" (Year One)

There were other times Elaine was frustrated. For example, the curriculum used *Hydra* as an exemplar organism, and she felt that her students, living near an ocean, should observe jellyfish instead "because they've seen jellyfish, they've probably been stung by them." (Year One)

Elaine realized her students needed to learn better how to structure, monitor, and demonstrate their learning. She did not blame them for their lack of study skills but tried to provide instruction related to biology. She explained:

> I was expecting them to know them, at first. And so that's why I think I didn't start out with a lot of planning to teach them how to take notes, or . . . how to write an essay, or even like test-taking strategies. . . . I try to help them figure out ways to approach problems. . . . How am I going to teach a kid to answer a science essay? That's the kind of thing I think about. (Year One)

Developing tests was hard for Elaine. Even though she used prepared questions from others, she modified them for her classes. She wanted students to apply their knowledge and reason things through. Typically, she was not satisfied with her testing procedures.

Deb: What kind of exams do you give? For the college prep?
Ela: Generally I give exams that I don't really like.
Deb: Well, none of us do.
Ela: I guess with a mixture of questions. There's these tests that go with the book, and sometimes I give parts of those.

Deb: Are they multiple choice?

Ela: Part multiple choice. I think the multiple choice on the tests are extremely difficult because they take the kids from where they are and jump five steps up. . . . I mean I try to help them build on thinking and using the facts and things they've learned to reason. But, I feel at times the questions are kind of obscure. So I cut and paste a lot. And I look around other books for questions that I like, because coming up with all my own, it feels kind of impossible when it comes around to doing the tests. (Year One)

Elaine believed that it was necessary to have a variety of questions "because it seems some kids do really well in one area, then do awfully in another area. And some kids are used to studying a certain way and others [another]." She explained:

I also give short answer [questions], and I generally try to have those deal with things we did in class that weren't in the book. And they have essays and usually I give them a choice of a couple that are related. [The tests are] usually pretty long, but I like to give a lot of questions just because I feel then the kids have more different areas that they're tested in and more different types of questions. (Year One)

When we talked the first year, Elaine's homework practices were in flux. "I used to have this philosophy that no one should have homework because I was thinking of all the issues that are involved in it." After talking with other new teachers and observing her students, Elaine gave assignments primarily because students expected them, even though "sometimes I give homework that I think is dumb, not a very good assignment." She had found that "it takes so much time for me to think up an assignment I'll be really proud to give. So I'll give reading and some questions."

Elaine tried different kinds of assignments and discovered some were easier to evaluate than others. She observed:

Sometimes I give concept maps. Sometimes I like doing concept maps as a group because kids make very shallow connections. And if you say, "Well, that's not really a great concept map," it's like, "But Miss Spring, I did everything that you said." Judging the concept map, I think you have to give them credit for doing [it].

I've had them do analogies, for example, between an atom and a cell, how is it similar, how is it different. Or make a chart and compare things, which I value because I think it helps them organize, compare, and see trends. (Year One)

Elaine's search for good lab activities that required students to think about the activity, was made more difficult by a new school requirement that students do open-ended labs. She elaborated:

> So I like them to write up either a summary or answer some questions or do graphing. And I had them do in the last few weeks probably three open-ended labs, because the department is saying that you should do one or two open-ended per marking period. I didn't even know how to find one, because the lab [book] that comes with the text has labs that really aren't open-ended. . . . [The department chair said], "If you're not sure, what you can do to have a lab that's open-ended is just have them change a variable." (Year One)

In retrospect, I should have asked Elaine more about what she felt open-ended labs should be and whether the department had any examples of open-ended labs available to the teachers.

PRACTICE AS A NEW TEACHER—YEAR TWO

In her second year of teaching, Elaine discussed projects that combined library research, a written report, and a presentation in front of the class. Elaine hoped these projects would offer students the chance to exercise ingenuity, but was not fully satisfied, even though "a lot of them like making posters, and really showing the information on it, not just drawing pictures." Elaine said there were problems with the oral presentations and I asked about nervousness. "They also have a hard time thinking out, 'Should you say these humongous words, if you don't know what they mean?' Even when I tell them not to, they still think they're important." Elaine thought about the presentations as we talked, expressing doubts and making an honest appraisal of her work.

Ela: So, I've got to work on the presentation type stuff. Because, personally, I was like "Why do we do this, Jim [department chair]? It doesn't make any sense. Do they really learn anything? I think they learn about their own topic . . . but I don't think most of them learn from the others."

Deb: Because?

Ela: I don't know. . . . I've been trying to think. What's a good thing to have kids investigate? . . . But some of the stuff that we're supposed to be teaching them, personally . . . I guess what it was, was [that] I was making them do a project because I didn't want to teach it! (laughs) . . . Which is not good—and I don't think I did that before-hand, but now I think, why did I give them a project in evolution? I don't know. (Year Two)

Elaine described a few new activities to help students develop good study skills and relate the biology content to life outside the class. One activity required them to find an article about genetics in a newspaper or news magazine and write a one-page summary. Elaine also required students to articulate and justify opinions about controversial topics in biology. What is intriguing is that she used this to help students not only learn to justify an opinion but learn that there is more than one justifiable opinion. I wish, though, I had asked her what she meant by a reasonable answer.

I sometimes have activities like "Should HIV testing be manda-tory?" That's not something that I'm going to test them on; I just want to develop their reasoning skills and their ability to see two sides to an issue. I sometimes will give test questions for things we've talked about that are very open-ended and they'll say, "But what do you want us to write?" and I say, "Well, just your opinion and some reasons backing it." . . . Some kids just leave it blank. And if they wrote something that was reasonable, I'd give them all the credit. (Year Two)

Elaine described another move she had made to address study skills but disparaged what she had done. I wonder now if she thought I wanted to learn only about completely new ideas or if she felt this assignment was only a prod to get them to read.

What I've done [new] this year was assign them to read something and outline or take notes on it and . . . then I sometimes say, you can use your notes and we'll have a quiz. . . . Which is nothing creative, but I think that there is a value to it, because I think there is a value to reading and there's no way those kids are going to take the book home unless there's something they have to write. (Year Two)

I asked Elaine if she had felt any pressure from her students to hand out study sheets or learning objectives. She replied:

It's kind of sad—but I don't think the majority of my students ask me to give them review questions. I'll say sometimes, for a test, these would be some good things to use as a resource to study, and they'll write down, "You should understand the difference between these two things," or "You should be able to explain this." But they don't really pressure me. (Year Two)

PRACTICE AS A NEW TEACHER—YEAR THREE

Elaine had worked with other teachers to revise the biology curriculum. I read through some of the topics they chose to cover, and Elaine's interpretation of these showed her emphasis on content related to humans and her desire to help students learn better. The curriculum work also shows how teachers can collaborate to provide a general outline yet still maintain personal freedom. She explained:

[Topics are] described in general ways and you can go down whatever path you want. Diversity of life, ecology, heredity, evolution, systems. . . . I spend kind of a lot of time on [systems], I know some people don't. I don't go into different [organisms] that much, I just like them to know the human body. Biological issues, disease, nutrition, and then common core skills, which involves sort of the process of doing science. And the bioethical issues one, I really like that one, and I find it interesting to find out how you're going to do that. (Year Three)

Elaine's students again had completed a project. They researched a disease, learning library research skills, and made posters, which were displayed in the classroom. The project fit into her curriculum and interests and appealed to students. Elaine again seemed to worry that telling me about a common exercise revealed her as less than creative, even though I tried to make clear I was most interested in how she structured the project.

Ela: I liked their posters, their presentations were all real interesting. I liked the reasons some kids chose topics.
Deb: Where'd you get the idea for—for how to structure it? I mean the idea of a disease report isn't really novel.
Ela: No, I didn't think any of it was very novel.
Deb: But how did you structure it so it worked in your class?
Ela: Well, where it fit in with the topic. We'd talked about the immune system, we'd done AIDS previously. I felt they really had some background to do it so they could feel comfortable reading about things. They seemed comfortable with the articles that they had. I checked out the resources ahead of time, which helped. I gave them

about 50 choices of diseases because I don't really think they would have been that creative, because they wouldn't have known about a lot [of diseases]. (Year Three)

By her third year Elaine was designing and using at least some activities that she liked. When she described an extended activity, one could see her ability to improvise, incorporate a key biological issue, relate it to students' lives, and learn about her students. This activity achieved many of her goals. She recalled:

I had them do [some standard] test, starting in class with physical activities, to tell which is dominant, your right or left [side]. For homework they had to do a written [standard] test with some different questions. Then, using a formula, they had to figure if they were right or left brain dominant or if they were whole brain.

They had to finish the test and write down the results and then explain if they thought it was a good test or not and why. . . . I got a lot of feedback about the test. So that was a more creative, open-ended type answer. They were able to give their own opinion about it.

They said, "Oh this test—is not working very well." I think I'll use it again, though, because a lot of them got [contradictory answers]. And we talked about why would you get [conflicting] results? . . . [A number said] they all stepped off with the same foot. And they're told in band to step off with your left. We talked about right and left handed.

And then Delmar was just into this. He said, "You know what, my mother thinks I'm going to be a science or math teacher, and I hate that stuff. I like music. Now I get it!". . . A girl wrote in her assignment that she argued that she was left-brained, and she went on about her reasoning, and said, "I speak another language." That might not be because she's left-brained, but . . . I just thought that was interesting because then I found out something else about her. And they like telling things like that, about their abilities, what they like.

And then Delmar brought up nature versus nurture, without knowing it. So I put that up on the board, and I said, "Delmar, you've just hit on one of the largest controversies in psychology, in biology." He's like, "Oh really?" (and we laugh at her tone of voice) "Yeah," I said, "nature versus nurture." And I described it and the kids are going, "Oh yeah, I've heard about that." (Year Three)

Elaine also had improved at finding and adapting laboratory exercises that would engage students, partly because she had now tried a number of different exercises and had learned how to implement ideas from other people. She still distinguished among different kinds of lab activities, with little emphasis on doing strict experiments.

> And, well, I guess there's different points of doing a lab. I like ones that are investigative. The chicken wing was more—it was a dissection but it was a follow-up on some ideas. I had some question inserted and then I had some things at the end that were more critical thinking. I felt it really worked well with what we were doing in class with tendons and ligaments, and bones and muscles and flexors and extensors. And then there's some labs that are more of an introduction. For example, the reaction time is the first thing we're doing with the nerves, so it starts them thinking about, "What does the nervous system do, why do we have—reflexes, why do we react?" (Year Three)

Developing good tests continued to be an issue for Elaine. "I probably use more objective [questions] than I would like, but I'm trying this year to find a few more ways I could make my life a little bit easier. And objective tests make it easier." Elaine did believe "some true–false and some multiple choice . . . can have kids analyze things a little." And, she found that developing good essay questions was not easy. "They just sort of come to me sometimes. Like one time we were doing the nervous system in one class, Richard Nixon had just died and so that really fit in with what we were doing."

Elaine again said she was finally comfortable not knowing everything and not being able to answer immediately all the questions students asked. "Before I was just really worried, are people going to think I don't know what I'm talking about?" She continued to question her ability to be creative, but was now comfortable enough to be more herself in class. Even in her third year, the enormity of the task of teaching was still daunting.

> And as a teacher I'm always looking for new ideas, and I'm always trying to get feedback on how students are learning so I can do a better job. 'Cause I still feel like I'm very critical of myself in terms of, "Are kids all involved here, or are they drifting off? Are they just glazing over?" I'm really concerned about that.
>
> I also just feel overwhelmed most of the time, and I'm always asking people for their secret of how to survive teaching without losing your mind. Because I feel like I continue to have that problem where I have all these ideas in my head and all these things I need to do and I can't zoom in on one. . . .

I wouldn't say I'm really creative in terms of coming up with these large—assignments that are really cool and so great. But I think I've become better at using resources and modifying. . . . And I'm really trying to make it so it's not [as if] we did something in September and we don't ever talk about it again.

And I don't get that sick feeling as much before class. The first year, before every class, I just felt sick, "Oh God, what's going to happen today?" And now I don't worry as much. . . . And people have told me before, you don't have to try [new things] all at once. But I always want to. (Year Three)

SUMMARY

Even as a student, Elaine was consistently clear about strategies she used in order to learn and to monitor her learning. She never thought that learning was, or should be, a quick or efficient process. She felt that she should be able to apply her knowledge to new situations or figure out problems. She used many of these criteria to monitor her students' work and recognized early that it was difficult to monitor someone else's comprehension. As a student, Elaine often presented herself as though she were confused and she struggled to act more confident. Student teaching caused her to see possible effects of her presentation on others and to work harder to modify her behaviors. As a teacher, she worked to help her students learn strategies for learning and for monitoring their learning.

Two factors—her realization that understanding is hard to determine, and her cooperating teacher's use of a range of assessment strategies—contributed to her desire to use a range of activities to foster and evaluate understanding. During her student teaching she also saw that assignments were necessary to encourage students to work and that some memorization was essential, but was not the final goal for learning. In student teaching she used observations of her students' work to evaluate her teaching, a practice she continued in her teaching.

Elaine had a consistent belief that learning biology should help students better understand themselves and their worlds. As a second- and third-year teacher, she also wanted her students to think about the ethical dimensions of controversial issues related to biology and to realize that there was more than one perspective on these issues. Elaine recognized different areas in biology and enjoyed applying theory.

As a student, Elaine articulated various purposes that could be served by laboratory work and as a teacher used laboratories that would serve these purposes. She rarely referred to using laboratory activities that explicitly modeled some aspect of experimental design. Although she never said so directly, it seemed that she viewed scientific thinking as systematic elimination of other explanations.

In her third year Elaine was literally and figuratively making her place in the school, as she had her own classroom and her own developed approach to biology teaching. She was using a range of assessment activities to enlarge her knowledge of student interests and how students learned, so that she could plan for the structure and topics they could benefit from most. It was only in her third-year interview that Elaine talked about the emotional demands of teaching and the stress she felt. She continued to pressure herself to come up with new and creative activities, but realized that many of her good activities would be modifications of existing materials and that it was unrealistic to think she could create a host of new things. She had not just mastered the subject matter of her teaching but by the third year had developed a coherent view of her course that included her concerns with ethical issues. Her sense of coherence seemed to allow her to react more immediately when her students brought up important topics spontaneously.

CHAPTER 6

Maggie Deering

I retain an image of Maggie at a TESM party. A basketball game started with men and women, but Maggie was the only woman who stayed in the thick of the game until it ended. Being completely unathletic, I felt that Maggie was a different kind of being. As much as I liked and respected her, during the study, I always felt a bit separate—older, fatter. Of course, I was older and fatter, but Maggie's athletic talents enhanced the contrast. I named Maggie after a childhood neighbor who was a serious and strong woman.

Maggie and George Frage belonged to a TESM cohort that seemed to be closer than others. We on faculty heard about regular Friday visits to a pub during student teaching, and the group organized a couple of graduation parties attended by most of the students. I supervised Maggie's student teaching, but did not teach the pre-student teaching seminar. Maggie student taught in a rural high school and worked with both the biology and chemistry teachers. One of these teachers was highly structured, with all lessons planned for the year, and the other was more flexible and let Maggie plan and present some of her own lessons.

Maggie taught for 2 years in a rural high school that served students from a range of economic backgrounds. Maggie taught Regents and non-Regents biology classes. She had her own classroom, which was well-equipped, clean, and organized, with an attached office area and room for storing materials.

After 2 years of teaching, Maggie moved and decided to use that time to take a year off from teaching to experience work in the private sector. She actually, though, found a position at a teacher center that provided in-service education for practicing teachers.

LEARNING

As a junior, Maggie believed learning was an active process, so she felt it was important that teachers present interesting content and use methods to engage learners. She believed teachers needed to be organized and to present material in different ways. She argued against requiring extensive memorization of terms, but did not have a fully explicated alternative to memorization. She spelled out conditions for good teaching:

> Presenting the material in a clear manner, trying to get students involved in a discussion or at least thinking about the material. I think often diagrams can help you visualize. And I think content choice can help a lot, too. Trying to present material that would be more interesting to the students so that they can relate to things. Or help them to relate it to more of their everyday experiences or things that they've already learned, in the class or other classes. Try to do things so you don't have to do a lot of memorization (she laughs). (Junior)

She did aver it was important to *apply* material learned, a point she made in her analysis of students she had tutored at Cornell. Some simply failed to do the work, but others said they had studied hard and learned all the material in their notes, but they still did poorly on tests. "They would get to the test and couldn't do the test. I think they would get too focused on the specific material and forget that you need to think about how it can relate to other situations."

Maggie had witnessed moments when she could tell that students she tutored understood because things suddenly made sense. "A lot of the times they'll just, as you're explaining, they'll start to get like, 'Oh, oh yeah, okay.'" However, she did not refer to using other means to determine their grasp of the material.

I asked Maggie what strategies she used for her own learning and she replied that although she had thought about this, she could not come up with a description of strategies she used. In fact, she said that if she tried to focus on *how* she was learning, she would forget to attend to *what* she was studying. "Every once in a while, I will notice . . . a light bulb will go on and I'll think, 'Oh yeah, this is like this.' And I can notice that I'm linking things. But generally—I'm not really sure . . . if there's anything specific, that I do."

In her senior-year interview, Maggie again distinguished between mere memorization and something else. She referred to conceptual learning, but provided no clear description of what this meant. Her characterization of the study of history, by the way, would cause historians some anguish. "History is not difficult conceptually; it's just a matter of reading and thinking about what's going on, but it's not something that's harder to understand . . . like genetics or chemistry."

Maggie again emphasized the importance of being able to apply one's knowledge; but in this interview she emphasized problem solving as the application. She also thought it important to learn to apply content to nonroutine problems.

Maggie continued to regard student interest as key and suggested that different content units might benefit from different teaching methods, but did not elaborate on this point. She saw the need for experimentation in her teaching, so that she could learn what would work best for her as a teacher.

> I think I'd like to start with sort of experimenting with different types of methods . . . doing things differently depending on the unit that you're doing and on what subject matter it is. I think that that will keep the greater variety in the classroom so that it doesn't get stale and boring. (Senior)

After student teaching, Maggie again stressed the need for variety in instruction, not just to avoid boredom but also to accommodate students' different approaches to learning and ensure success for more students. In this interview Maggie did not relate teaching method to the aspect of biology studied, even though I asked about this directly.

> *Deb:* I know a lot of people who don't vary methods regardless of the content.
> *Maggie:* I think I would just get bored. . . . Especially since there is so much research about how students learn better in some methods and worse in others. So I think if you vary the method at least you've hopefully hit upon the best ways. (MAT)

After student teaching, Maggie was more explicit about her learning strategies. She said she worked to identify the big ideas, the important concepts, and had noticed that doing so enabled her to understand and take notes better. However, Maggie had some doubts about her learning, possibly because she thought that learning could and should be done expeditiously.

> *Maggie:* I think I actually have changed how I learn since I've been in the [TESM] program because I am more conscious about how I am thinking. . . . I mean, I think I definitely try and pick out the more important concepts and find it easier to get concepts and notes. I don't think I'm an extremely quick learner partly because I don't always have a real good concentration. I'm a learner who can't put everything aside except for one [thing].

Deb: Why do you think it's good to have . . . that kind of concentration?
Maggie: Well, I think a lot of it is just that it's much more efficient and if I could do that, I think that then I would be able to sit down and get the work done. And then take the break that would help me feel better and more relaxed to enjoy life so that I can then sit down and do the next thing. (MAT)

Maggie could not memorize readily. "Things like new vocabulary words, I can forget very easily, even if I understand the concept." She criticized a teacher she observed who seemed to stress memorization rather than learning concepts. Maggie's notion of concept seemed to include overarching principles, although she was vague. One teacher required students to go over and over the material until it was memorized. "Whereas if they were to think more about the concepts and how the concepts are related, they might have to remember fewer things and remember how they are related. Then they can remember, hopefully, for a longer time."

Maggie worked with students who did not ask questions in class, which troubled her. She initially thought they understood the material so well that they were bored, but tutoring showed "they were just so confused that they were frustrated. And bored with it probably because they were so confused." She realized then that she would need to learn ways to monitor understanding in class and seemed quite comfortable when I said there was no one best way to determine understanding.

Maggie: I mean sometimes it is just from the questions that you ask them. Do you use this style or do you do that? I guess that would probably be the way to ask them some questions.
Deb: There is no best way.
Maggie: True, you know, sometimes through phrases or lab reports.

When I asked Maggie how she would like to improve, she mentioned she had asked her students for feedback to learn what she needed to improve:

I think the first thing I would do is to try to find a totally new way to approach [a topic]. Because that was something that some of my chemistry students actually said to me in my evaluations, that I explain things the same way. (MAT)

After her student teaching Maggie was more critical of university teachers and planned to spend less time lecturing:

I have noticed that a couple of the professors who did lectures in the class that I worked with would . . . start moving really quickly with the information they were giving to the students and just keep going [and skip the break]. The professors would be so excited about what they were talking about, whereas the students are just sort of sitting there sleeping. I think that made me realize, too, that in a lot of ways it is a lot more fun to teach the material than to sit and try to listen and learn the material. (MAT)

BIOLOGY

During her junior-year interview Maggie characterized biology as a practical discipline with applications to humans. She believed that learning biology should help learners develop a greater awareness of and appreciation for the natural world and believed that there were some things in biology that were just inherently fascinating, even though they had no direct application to humans. Maggie thought that learning about these interesting things could make study of the science seem less exclusive.

In my animal behavior class they showed a lot of interesting behaviors, like Professor Eisner's bombardier beetles that shoot out hydroquinones. And something like that is just sort of awe-inspiring and I think that presenting some things like that, every once in a while [is good]. . . . So that biology doesn't seem like just this intellectual science that's just for these people in [specialized] kinds of things. So it's something that they realize that can actually affect them in their life and there is a need for biology, that it is in medical research and that all these different organisms are just as important as we are. That even little bombardier beetles are important. (Junior)

When I asked her, Maggie offered several reasons for her love of biology, one of which resonated with her wish to make biology seem a less exclusive discipline:

I think part of it was because I always loved animals. When I got into high school I always enjoyed my science. I think part of it was doing problems. . . . I think another reason, this might sound kind of funny, but I think also because it was a very like nonfeminine kind of thing? It was kind of like, "Oh well yeah, we've got to, women have to get out there and work, being scientists and researchers and show that we can do this stuff." (Junior)

Maggie emphasized the importance of understanding biological mechanisms and the dynamic nature of knowledge in science. Her view of the humanities was a bit cursory, as was her description of research.

Maggie: As opposed to other things like history or English I guess I
would think of [biology] as more of a practical discipline. You're
learning about the world around you. And some things that you can
use, as opposed to something like English where you're—learning
about lots of stories that are (laughs) more or less just for your
enjoyment. So in that respect it's something that you can use and it
is a science, there's a lot of research.
Deb: What does research in science consist of?
Maggie: Uh, doing experiments, doing observations, field studies. Trying
to learn new information about the way things work. (Junior)

Maggie felt that biology class in high school served as "sort of an introduction to science. I think that that might be one reason why they put it before chemistry and physics." She felt that the practical aspects of biology would "inform students who may not be going on into the sciences about different aspects of their own body."

In her senior-year interview Maggie referred to branches of biology that used different research approaches and made different kinds of claims:

If you look at something like genetics compared to something like
ecology or evolution, you have to . . . approach it differently. . . . In
evolution we're often looking at fossils that don't exist anymore.
Sometimes you can combine the approaches. (Senior)

LABORATORY INSTRUCTION

Maggie stressed that laboratory exercises in her biology classes aided the learning of content and skills. She also felt labs could increase student engagement because they provided an enjoyable alternative to lectures.

Deb: What do you see as important about having labs in biology?
Maggie: I think being able to visualize things, definitely. When I took
[the Cornell class on] vertebrates we did a lot of dissections and I
never would have learned all that material if we hadn't done lab.
Also I think you can get a lot of manual type skills through lab. I'm
learning how to etherize *Drosophila*. And I think because it's something that tends to be a little more enjoyable for the students, they
often will pay more attention. (Junior)

Maggie offered the standard criticism of cookbook labs she had experienced. She thought that labs could help students learn about scientific investigation, but did not stress mastering a method. Instead, she pointed out that frustration is often part of a scientific investigation, and students could experience some of that. In order to have this experience one would have to discard the typical lab exercise that has known outcomes. She reflected:

> Sometimes I think if you have labs that . . . might even tend to fail more, it's a little bit more frustrating but I think that helps the students to see what science is about, a little bit more. . . . I guess I haven't really thought about labs, as much, for what you can actually do in a lab. I've thought about them more as why they can be useful. (Junior)

After student teaching she continued to emphasize that good labs would engage students, and noted that many different kinds of activities were called labs.

PRACTICE AS A NEW TEACHER—YEAR ONE

Maggie was not hired for her first job until August and felt that her opportunities to plan were curtailed. She felt that as a new teacher she had good support from colleagues because she could rely on them to help her plan her classes. The biology teachers used all of the same lab exercises so she did not have to design her own. Maggie said her first year was hard for her and planned changes to make. Many of her plans were influenced by her desire to foster students' engagement with the material and to help them develop the skills she felt that they needed for learning.

Deb: How much did you end up writing your own [materials]?
Maggie: Not as much as I would have liked. (laugh) I did start writing some worksheets on my own, which I just would write out by hand.
Deb: What do you mean by worksheet?
Maggie: Well, having questions for the kids to fill in, that we would work on either in class or as homework. . . . I'd try to get them with some thinking questions, but also sometimes just general questions. For example, if we did the respiratory system, "What are the alveoli?" . . . Or, "What is the function of the structure?" and have them write out something that would help them focus from the reading. Because a lot of them have trouble finding information in the book. (Year One).

Maggie appreciated that she could use labs used by the other teachers, but was not satisfied because the students "didn't have to write up any sort of lab report or conclusions. And I'd like to start doing that next year." She and another new teacher had some released time to develop new labs, some of which were based on labs that they remembered doing in high school.

Maggie began her year by using an experienced teacher's tests, but eventually developed her own because she felt the tests focused primarily on the recall of memorized terms. Maggie included multiple choice questions on her tests to prepare her students for the Regents exams, but added questions that would require students to compose answers.

> I'm sort of making up my own tests, taking questions from the teacher resource material and from old Regents exams, so that they would have those kind of questions. And I usually tried to have part multiple choice and then some short answer questions, that they had to write things down. (Year One)

Maggie learned that her students did not write well, and wanted them to improve. She also wanted them better prepared for the writing segments that were on the Regents exams. The following quote shows the tension between using writing to communicate ideas and thinking, and the criteria for writing imposed by the external Regents examination. I do not think I helped Maggie examine this tension when we talked, because I failed to see it at the time. She explained:

> And that's something that I want to focus more on next year, getting them to do complete sentences. . . . I'd like to start emphasizing earlier, and I'm not sure exactly how. That's one of my questions for you. This year I tried putting comments on their tests, to help them [learn] how to answer more, but I didn't take points off. Whereas I might try next year doing something, maybe not a test, but a quiz that's a worksheet, where they have to do a considerable amount of writing. Where I can go back and give them a lot of suggestions and really grade them hard on that so that then I can hopefully have them doing a little better for the test. (Year One)

Maggie attempted to engage students in discussions about the material as an alternative to lecturing. By using discussions, she did not always cover material in the same way in each class, which led to problems with the content validity of her test questions. "I found it hard to coordinate trying to write questions exactly the way you've covered them in class or something, because you might cover it a little bit differently in each class."

When I asked Maggie how her tests were working, her analysis revealed her awareness of the complexities of teaching. She had considered possible explanations for student behaviors, analyzed the kinds of thinking she expected of students, and contrasted this with their expectations. Her response suggests ways she could modify her testing to conform better to student expectations and how she could prepare them to meet her expectations.

Deb: How do they work, the tests?

Maggie: That was something I found was hard to evaluate because a lot of my students didn't do very well on tests. But I don't know if it's because I wasn't teaching the material well enough—which I think is probably part of it, just being new—or if it was partly because they weren't putting enough time and effort in studying, which I think was also a lot of it. (laughs) Or if it was because I was just making the tests too difficult for them. You can't really experiment because there are too many variables! (laughs) . . . I did notice that oftentimes I was using questions that were more synthesis type of things, or ones where they had to apply things. And I probably didn't have enough of the vocabulary type questions. I think it might work if I did a little more work with them, before the test, on some of that. (Year One)

I asked her about her plans for the next year. Maggie hoped to find ways to get students more actively engaged and making connections, and spoke about developing her knowledge of biology. She also noted the personal pressures she felt as a teacher:

Definitely I would like to have more examples that the students can relate to (rising inflection). . . . I'm sure there are a lot of examples that I already know, but as you're trying to prepare for things, this first year, it's like you don't have time to think about anything you're doing (rising inflection). You don't have time to come up with creative ways of doing things.

And I would like to be able to do some more projects. We did a simple project in the general biology class where they had to make a model of a flower and label the different parts. That worked very well. So maybe some things like that, where rather than having a quiz on the different parts of the flower, they might have to make a model of the flower. (Year One)

PRACTICE AS A NEW TEACHER—YEAR TWO

Maggie continued modifying exercises and experimenting with different kinds of activities. When I visited, her general biology class was working on a project on bovine growth hormone (BGH). Students had to prepare a poster showing what BGH was and then draft a letter to the editor that argued for or against allowing farmers to use BGH. This project was consistent with her desire that students view biology as practical, with connections to everyday life. It also provided these students the chance to communicate their understandings in a public form and the opportunity to take a position on a controversial issue that represented an ill-structured problem.

Deb: And you said the general kids really like the bovine growth
hormone project. I could see that today, they got into it.
Maggie: When I first introduced it [the activity], they were saying, "Oh,
this is stupid, I don't care about cows." But I think once they got
into the assessment part where they had to actually do the letter,
and they had to think a little bit more about how can this really
impact on me, and they see [articles on BGH] in the paper on their
own, that they got into it.

Planning for the project was time-consuming:

Well, part of it is just more think time, thinking about how am I
going to structure it, so that I know that I can keep them on task,
and give them something to do that they will understand what they
need to do.
Part of it was involved in collecting the articles, . . . copying
them . . . figuring which ones to give them. There is time involved in
making up the objective sheet, and the vocabulary sheets. Then
making up the worksheets and the questions for that. And typing
out the whole assessment sheet, which I know that most of them
didn't read very much (laugh) but I want to be sure to have it there
so that if they had questions I could show them on the sheet. . . . The
BGH project has worked really nicely this year because it's right in
the media, now! But it's not one that I think I would be able to do
again, before very long, because it won't have the same sort of
appeal, once it's no longer a real controversy. (Year Two)

In her second year, Maggie remained ambivalent about lecturing. She
noted that some students did not stay focused during lecture and there-

fore had difficulties, but factors pushed her to lecture. Factors she identified as salient included the students' inability to read and grasp the textbook, the pressure of the Regents examination, her need for consistency from class to class, and student resistance to discussion.

Maggie returned to her own high school experiences when she talked about her dilemma, perhaps because she had not worked through it for herself:

> That's one of the reasons why I think the notes don't work. Because they just blindly write down what I have up there and they don't really think about what it means. And I remember vividly, when I was in high school, my history class, freshman and sophomore year. In freshman year the notes were given to us. They were all just straight outline notes. And then in the sophomore year in history class, he . . . wrote a few words on the board, but everything else was done by discussion and he spent some time at the beginning of the year sort of teaching us how to take notes from the discussion.
>
> But in order to do that [discussion in class] I would have to be sure that they had done the reading first. [But] their textbook has so much information that's beyond what we cover, and has so much vocabulary, that a lot of them find it difficult to read and wouldn't know what to focus on. (Year Two)

Maggie tried more projects in her second year of teaching, in both the Regents and non-Regents classes. One required students to make a model of a cell using materials that would be analogous to the different parts of the cell. Maggie enhanced the project by using it to provide an occasion for writing. Maggie had a thorough analysis of how the project worked and how she might improve its structure. She again clarified the kind of thinking students should have done.

Maggie: And it worked pretty nicely, except that in my Regents class I didn't spend quite as much time discussing the models in class. First, because I thought they'd learn some more of this as they do the model (rising inflection). But then I found that for a lot of them, they didn't think enough about the functions of the parts. So a lot of them made analogies like jello to represent cytoplasm, because they're similar in texture. Or noodles to represent the mitochondria because they're similar in shape. Whereas I gave a couple of examples of things like a battery might be like a mitochondrion because it provides energy.

Deb: Oh, it's a functional analogy!

Maggie: Right. And some of them did that sort of thing. But I need to change it a little bit to kind of force them so that at least three analogies are by function and three are by structure, or something like that. . . . The other part they had to do for it was a write up where they had to describe what represented their cell part, and then why it represented that. And that's where they had trouble, because a lot of them could write what represented it, but they didn't describe why. . . . And some of them I think didn't really think enough about why it represented it. And so that's something that I want to try to develop a little more. (Year Two)

Maggie continued to use a combination of different kinds of questions on exams, and again provided vocabulary sheets for students to complete. The worksheets served to keep some students busy in class while others finished exams, but in this interview she was unsure of the value of the vocabulary sheets. She observed:

I don't think they learn a whole lot from just writing the definitions down. I think it helps a little so that they get the introduction. I think a lot of it is that they just copy the words and don't think about it. But I think it helps a little and it gives them something to go back to, to study from (rising inflection). (Year Two)

In her first year of teaching, Maggie had a number of students who failed the Regents examination by just a small margin. As a second year teacher, she decided to give students a midyear quiz using only questions from former Regents examinations, an idea suggested by other teachers. She described how the students performed:

Ah, not real well, but okay, considering that it was only halfway through [the year] and some of the questions were things that we had covered, but a lot of the stuff gets covered again, over and over. (Year Two)

I really do wonder what was going on here. Maggie obviously was responding to the need to train her students to do better on the Regents exam. But what did it mean that some topics would be covered several times? Was she using the existing Regents curriculum structure to organize units, so that the repetition was built in, or did she feel that there were certain key concepts that would be relevant to several units and thereby revisited? Would Maggie have reorganized the units in the Regents curriculum to decrease the redundancy, or would there have been pressure at the school to stay with the Regents curricular organization? Perhaps her discussion of objectives suggests that she might have done work to reorganize the Regents curriculum but that she felt she had little latitude for change. Maggie had developed objectives for her non-Regents students and had begun to develop objectives for the Regents units.

Maggie: Well, I have been giving them to the Regents students now. But I haven't had to put very much thought into the objectives for the Regents, because—most of the objectives are pretty much spelled out for us. It's a highly content based course, so it's tougher to focus on skills. Most of the objectives that get written are [related to] what content do they need to know. . . . I'm kind of writing them up almost more at the end of the unit, so I can go back and make sure, "Okay, have I covered everything I need to?" I'm writing them up, giving them to them as a review.

Deb: And a thing for studying?

Maggie: Right. And I've been putting some practice questions on the bottom because some of the students asked for questions, which is working okay. They've also been asking, "How come we get these at the end of the unit?"

Deb: Well, next year if you were to teach—

Maggie: Right. This is the first year I've been doing this, I'm still busy making things up, and I'm going to try to get them out at the beginning of the unit. For the unit we're doing now, I was able to do that. (Year Two)

Maggie had begun writing the objectives for the general biology class after attending an in-service workshop on effective teaching. She found that even after some practice in class, the students still did not do well on examinations. She speculated, "That's partly because I've been trying to ask . . . some of the higher-level, thinking-type questions. Compare and contrast, or a lot with structure and function or application-type questions."

I asked her what she would like to be as a teacher in 3 to 5 years. Maggie continued to wish to design activities to engage students but also referred to the demands that teaching placed on her:

I would like to be able to do a lot more hands-on stuff. More of the projects similar to the BGH project because it's also, I think, more exciting to do that sort of thing, you see more of the enthusiasm of the students and see all the different responses. But I would like to do it with having enough time to plan for those, without going nuts. I'd like to be able to have a little bit more time, to relax at the end of the day. Or sleep. (Year Two)

SUMMARY

As a junior, Maggie could not articulate strategies she used to learn and monitor her learning, but knew that there were times when she suddenly understood. She also had seen such moments when she tutored, but did not know what led to these. By the time of her student teaching interview she mentioned strategies she used to learn and also some anxieties she had about her own learning. It seems she felt there was some technique or strategy for learning faster that she had not yet learned. She knew that learning was more than memorization, but it was only after she began teaching that she articulated some of the processes involved in understanding.

Although Maggie spoke of the importance of varying teaching approaches before she began full-time teaching, she offered little detail about different approaches. Her experiences with one cooperating teacher and at the university after her student teaching convinced her she did not want to lecture, and she actually experimented with not giving lectures in her first year of teaching. The experiment was not successful for a number of reasons, so she adopted a more traditional approach to lecturing in her second year.

In student teaching, Maggie used feedback from her students to learn that she needed to develop more than one way to explain material. Her concern with finding good examples persisted after her first year of teaching, during which time she felt nearly overwhelmed by the need to cover the prescribed Regents curriculum.

Maggie viewed biology as both fascinating and practical but did not express a commitment to having her students learn any particular material. She considered that understanding human biology and topics related to human interests was important for high school students. In some of her interviews she referred to different areas of study in biology. Ironically, as a preservice teacher Maggie had emphasized that student interest in the material was important to learning, but in our conversations in her first years of teaching Maggie did not refer to Regents students' interest in the material, probably because the content was dictated by the external examination and she was still learning how to present and structure that content.

Maggie had little to say about laboratory teaching in her early interviews, other than to say that laboratory exercises could help students learn content and skills. As a teacher, she worked to develop lab activities that would engender thinking about the material rather than merely following procedures.

Maggie received help from other teachers, but even in her first year began to move away from the kind of testing and labs that the more experienced teachers used. In her second year she tried new activities in her classes that called for higher-level thinking and explanatory writing, and realized students needed more explicit instruction in these areas. She collected evidence about how well activities worked and had ideas about better ways to structure the activities she used. Because of the press to ensure a higher passing rate on the Regents examination, Maggie was developing ways to train her students for the exam. She provided objectives and practice exams to help her students master the Regents material.

Maggie's second year was easier than the first but she found there were still many problems to address.

When Maggie read the full case study and introduction, she wrote me a two-page e-mail. Her remarks included:

> I got your lengthy case study and thoroughly enjoyed reading it. Many times I read my comments, especially from early in the program, and thought to myself, "I said THAT?" It was really interesting seeing how my ideas have, or have not, changed. It was like re-reading a journal that I didn't have to take the time to write. Thanks for writing it for me! . . . I work a lot with veteran teachers . . . so I've been thinking, "What else about teaching and teachers might I be making assumptions about?" I've always thought of teachers as being reflective. . . . I'm not so sure that all teachers are. As I read your case study about me, I wondered if my involvement in the project helped me be more reflective in my practice. . . . The interviews with you seemed to me like another part of the teacher ed program. I thought it was really interesting seeing how I answered the same questions differently during the years of my development. I think there would be merit in including something similar in the teacher ed program. Obviously you don't want to have to conduct and transcribe interviews with all the TESM students, but maybe journal assignments that would require students to reflect on the same questions each year would be helpful. Anyway, just a thought.

And, after correcting some details, she added: "I just want you to know that I'm old and fat now too . . . I haven't played basketball in at least a year, but it is hard to find people who play at the same slow pace as I!"

CHAPTER 7

George Frage

I interviewed George when he was still a student in my course, something I had done with none of the other new teachers. I had assured him I would not listen to or analyze the interview until after the semester ended, and that what he said in the interview would not influence his grade at all. He did not seem bothered. George enjoyed his course at Shoals so much that he worked there for the next two summers. George did his student teaching in a local high school and worked with one of the best-known teachers at the school. I did not supervise his student teaching, nor did I teach the pre-student teaching seminar for his cohort. In his first year of teaching, George taught a nearly full load at a private and prestigious eastern preparatory school. Most of the students lived on campus, as did George. He taught two levels of biology classes at this school. In his second year of teaching, George worked at another private eastern preparatory school, smaller than the first. George again lived in the residences on campus. When I visited him in his second year, George was teaching high school chemistry and biology classes. George did not have one classroom to which he was assigned at either school, but moved to different rooms. He had office space in the departmental area. After 2 years of teaching, George returned to graduate school, to complete a research degree in biology. I chose George's last name, Frage, after the German word for question. Once I had chosen that, the name George, especially with the German pronunciation, provided a nice sound, with the same rhythm as Georg Solti.

LEARNING

George viewed memorization as one step to learning. "In biology there's a lot of memorization, just things and concepts." He studied by reviewing material and rephrasing until "something clicked." When I asked him about his own learning, George explained what he did to learn and believed it was important to understand mechanisms and their applications:

Okay. Umm—I try to think of myself as an active learner, not just someone who sits there and tries to memorize everything. I like to strip everything down, and find out what's underneath it, and how it applies, to myself, and how I can use it. I'm turned off to just learning for learning's sake. Learning is just kind of fun. I think that's one of the biggest things that you should learn, is learn how to learn—if you're not going to learn learning, you'll have a hard time every time something new comes up. . . . I don't like to learn things superficially. (Junior)

His wish to learn deeply led George to be critical of conditions he perceived at Cornell:

That's why the work load here kind of turns me off. Because in a lot of my classes I would really like to get in depth, instead of covering a million things just to cover them. And not just in science. Like in German or English or something like that. I would like to look up every word I don't understand, and then maybe have time to memorize a list of words every day, or something that I didn't know. It just seems like the faster you go, the more material you try to learn in a certain amount of time, you know, it reaches a limit. And I think we're past the limit here at Cornell, where it just starts to hinder. (Junior)

George believed that it was necessary to develop a larger framework when learning, to make connections and fit ideas into some big picture, although he was unsure how a teacher could stimulate the process.

I'm not sure exactly how it [good teaching] should be done, but I have ideas about what it should . . . bring out in students. First of all they should learn the subject matter and they should have a Grand Scheme of things. Because I think a lot of students, just [say], "Okay, now we're doing amphibians." And they do that and they file it off somewhere and then, "Now we're doing this," and they never bring it all together. (Junior)

George had loved his seventh-grade life science class and "couldn't wait to take the real biology in high school. I was never intimidated by science like I hear a lot of people are."

When I asked him how he'd gauge students' understanding, he presented a relatively straightforward process. He noted that students might not answer honestly, but did not speculate why:

Well, first I ask the obvious, "Is that clear? Did you get that?" And, you know, they'll most always say "Yes," whether they do or not. And then (laughter) a lot of times I'll say, "Well, explain it back to me, to make sure you have it right." And that pretty much does it. If they can explain it, obviously they understand it. (Junior)

In his interview after student teaching, George returned to the idea that learning biology involves understanding mechanisms underlying phenomena and requires making connections across units and topics. George's description of his learning illustrates the care he took to express his thoughts fully and his readiness to quell my interruption of this thinking.

George: Well, on the negative side, I think I'm kind of a slow learner. But a good learner. There are a lot of things that I won't pick up quickly. . . . And I think that has to do with how I learn because I tend to synthesize things, I think, perhaps more than other people who learn quickly or when I'm learning quickly.

Deb: So you've had some experiences of learning quickly?

George: I'm not quite sure what I meant by that. Let me finish this thought.

Deb: Okay. Sorry.

George: So I think I learn slowly because there's a lot going on up there (points to head) not because I'm like mentally incapable or something like that. (chuckles) And when I finally do learn it, it seems like it's there, for a while. (MAT)

BIOLOGY

George clearly loved the study of biology. I asked him what it was about biology that "got him hooked," and he replied, "I don't know. It's just so complex, and just so wonderful." He went on to say that he was not as excited in his advanced biology classes, which were narrowly focused, even though he did well. But, he found that "now that I'm tutoring in [freshman] biology, I just eat up that lecture. And the excitement is back again." George also pointed out that the material in introductory biology made sense to him because he was reviewing the material, and thought it must be confusing and frustrating for students covering the material for the first time.

When I asked him to characterize biology, George revealed a complex understanding of the discipline, noting that the field could be approached from many perspectives and that biological knowledge continued to develop.

I don't know. Science has always been labeled as being more
"objective" than, say, the humanities and English and history and
things like that. I don't know if that's true so much with biology,
just because there's just so much. It's very subjective, what part you
focus on and how you interpret it if you don't know the whole
picture, which you don't right now. . . . I think biology's kind of an
intermediate between, say, the pure sciences such as physics and
chemistry, and the humanities. Just because it's so rich. . . . I mean,
it's made up of chemistry and physics and all that, but it has a lot
more concepts—a lot of those things that just are. (Junior)

George did not state a unique reason to learn any particular aspect of
biology. "I've always been so excited about biology that I've never really
thought about biology as something that everyone should have, for some
social reason." He felt that it was possible that learning biology could contribute to an individual's ability to participate in public life because of an
increased understanding of the world, but was more concerned that students in biology classes learn to think. "I think it's just one step in your
education where you're taught to think for yourself. To think about what's
going on around you."

George questioned the amount of detail he was required to learn in
some of his biology classes and extrapolated his reaction to his future in
teaching. "In the back of my head I hear them saying, 'Now, Mr. Frage, why
do we ever have to know this?' And you know sometimes I can't find an
answer in there."

After his student teaching George said he had been frustrated by the
style and amount of lecturing he felt required to do, and continued to hope
that students would learn that science knowledge continued to evolve. He
explained what he wanted to do.

When I'm lecturing, not just answer questions but bring up a lot
of questions. I think science would be pretty anticlimactic if it
just answered questions, if the lecturer just got up there and talked
for 45 minutes and everything were crystal clear. If you're thinking actively about what the person's saying, it should be answer-
ing a lot of things but also bringing up whole new questions.
(MAT)

George continued to insist that there was no essential biology content
crucial to teach in a high school class, that biology class should teach people
to think "in some sort of rational way. In some sort of disciplined way, some
sort of testable . . . scientific way."

LABORATORY INSTRUCTION

George criticized prescribed laboratory activities because they failed to address the thought needed to begin any experiment and therefore did not teach students scientific thinking.

> Because most of the labs are classic experiments that have already been done, so there isn't that initial thinking process of, "How am I going to solve this problem and find out how this really works?" . . . It's missing the vital thought process at the beginning, which is part of the scientific method. (Junior)

George remained critical of standard labs after his student teaching. He thought students should develop their own labs, similar those done in the adaptations course at Shoals, but seemed ambivalent about the role of specific content knowledge.

> Ideally they'd come up with their own questions to answer and then try to answer them. But even in "Adapts" we don't do that. It's all kind of loaded. They give you a lecture on zonation, [for example]. So it's kind of limited to that. You can't say, "I want to study the relationship of sponges to anemones." (MAT)

George did not think lab activities should be used to help students learn content, even though they often were. Nor should students follow procedures with known outcomes. He posed criteria for labs to foster thinking, but knew such labs were rare.

> I think ideally what [labs] should be doing is, I guess I'll use the buzz word, pose some discrepant event that serves as a launching pad for them to start thinking about a certain problem—I mean if a lab totally makes sense from beginning to end, it probably wasn't worth doing. I think they should be somewhat puzzled through- out . . . by some of the things that are going on. (MAT)

George's belief that learners should synthesize and apply their knowl- edge was evident in a description of a 2-day lab exercise done in his stu- dent teaching. The work did not address the hypothesis-generating or testing aspects of investigation, but did involve some of his ideas about learning and addressed the difficulties of identifying causes in biology. He described the exercise:

Well, it's a lab on the effect of oil spills on seabirds. The students make their own little oil spills. . . . I collected some gull feathers. Students learn a little bit about feathers and their structure and function. They draw feathers and stuff like that. They squirt water on the feathers and then describe what happens. The feathers are totally water repellent because of the [natural] oil on them.

Then they dunk the feathers in the [oil slick] and the feathers totally lose their shape. Then . . . they clean them with a detergent solution, and the feathers actually get almost totally clean. But then after that, they test for water repellency. And the feathers aren't, anymore. Because not only did you remove the motor oil but you removed the natural oils that keep them water repellent.

After the work with feathers, George showed a movie on the Exxon Valdez oil spill, then had small groups identify the causes of the spill and present to the class. George's description illustrated his hopes to stimulate students' thinking beyond the superficial and to engage their emotions.

And it was just the most amazing thing because they're just so into it, and it just really touched them. . . . They were just really thinking. I told them . . . when they think of a cause, go one deeper than that. It's easy to say . . . , "Well, the captain was drunk, so they hit a reef." "Why was the captain drunk?" "Because he drank alcohol." (laughs) But they got into things like dependence on fossil fuels for power and the problem with just having so many boats in the water that it's inevitable that they are going to sink and crash and leak. . . . And they were just talking about that and some of the groups were just thanking us for this. They're like, "Those people don't care about this!" It was such a feel-good day. (MAT)

PRACTICE AS A NEW TEACHER—YEAR ONE

When I visited George he was behind schedule so was giving lectures on the material. Students asked many questions, and he asked questions of them. George said he worked to help students develop an awareness of the big picture.

We were about to embark on all the different systems of the body, which are all each in a different chapter and discreet unit. The message is that they are all operating independently of one another, that there's really no connection between them. And so the first thing I had them do was make a concept map of all the different systems and how they're interrelated. (Year One)

George had to present the material that was included on the departmental final, which also would likely appear on the achievement tests these students would take for college admission. He tried to ensure students would take an active role in learning, to decrease his need to lecture.

Deb: It seemed to me that you had them do reading before lecture, and then your lecture is a discussion, a clarification, a making-sure-they-get-it.

George: That's usually the intention. Sometimes just time-wise it ends up inverting; I end up assigning the reading after I've talked about it. Sometimes I assign it twice, before and then after discussion. (Year One)

George hated to ignore student questions that related to the content. These questions intrigued him and also helped him realize things he did not know. He seemed undisturbed that he did not know the answers immediately.

I actually started something this year because I find that a lot of kids were asking questions that were great questions, about the material, and I'd say, "I don't know the answer. But that's a great question." So I started a practice of writing them up on the right-hand corner of the board, and then I have a little book of questions that I transcribe them into. And then they usually sit there a week or two and then I try to find answers for them. (Year One)

George began the year designing tests with essay questions and no multiple choice questions, but soon found it took him too long to grade those tests, so he compromised. George felt he needed to help students study because students who did poorly "weren't good at pulling things out of the text . . . at realizing which parts of the text are the most important." He prepared review sheets for the tests that he thought would most help "the students who aren't good at reading my mind."

Deb: Oh, study questions. (I read some aloud) "What's the point of having a nervous system? Do all animals have one?" "Compare and contrast nervous and endocrine systems."

George: See, I started off the year with tests like this. And I have drifted away from that for two reasons. . . . It was taking me a year and a day to correct them. I found that I can get away with these [questions] if . . . I don't leave much room for interpretation and I know exactly what they're going to write. . . . I mean, you'd like to give them questions that they're going to interpret, make, answer in their own way.

Deb: But you also have to live.

George: Right. Exactly. And also, I've started adding multiple choice questions because the finals are multiple choice and they would just be blown away with 50 multiple choice questions when they haven't had one. So I give in with the multiple choice.

George had done some lab projects that took a significant amount of time and slowed down progress through the curriculum. These projects, which he "would love to do the entire year," enabled students to develop their own hypotheses and a way to test them. He used the model from the Adaptations course, ensuring students had background knowledge for the work, but did not stress the importance of this knowledge. George stressed he would like to "just throw all the subject matter in the trash bin." One project came during the unit on the circulatory system. Groups chose factors that might affect pulse rate that they would investigate. The groups chose temperature and exercise, then as a class designed and ran a test and collected data.

To evaluate students' work on this project, George looked at the organization of their reports, but focused most on their data analysis, emphasizing his experimental approach to research.

I'm pretty harsh on the graphs because they are usually the turning point for the report. If the graphs are bad, then the discussion is often not good. . . . Those who made appropriate graphs that showed trends in the data, ended up writing really clear discussion sections about the effects of certain variables on what we're looking at. (Year One)

PRACTICE AS A NEW TEACHER—YEAR TWO

At his new school, George had started the year handing out review sheets for his tests but by the middle of the year stopped the practice because it was not working.

George: They could do the problems on the review sheet and answer those questions to the letter, and then on the test, they wouldn't be able to do anything because they would be slightly different from the review sheet. . . . And they do fine now [without review sheets]. I don't know if it actually improved because the tests are different, but they're not struggling without the review sheets.

Deb: That's the other joy of teaching, that there are so many variables that you never figure it out.

George: Exactly. (Year Two)

George's new school was much smaller, and emphasized individual responsibility and allowed students more control over school life. George found his students had tried to avoid working independently. "And I'm realizing now that I've just been had a lot of times. They're just not doing the work at home, they're expecting you to teach every little thing to them in class and if that doesn't happen then it's unfair to have a test."

George had students prepare posters and do class presentations. He had used these his first year, but we had not discussed them. George thought that the projects were generally successful and mentioned the excitement shown by many students, "and that was great, for them to actually take charge of their own learning."

George experimented with a take-home test to avoid lecturing on straightforward material. The test structure required students to work independently but also emphasized the importance of taking good notes in class, an apparent contradiction that made sense when I realized he lectured on the more complex material.

> I think plant anatomy is one of the most boring subjects, so we didn't spend all our time looking at cross-sections of monocot and dicot stems and what not. I focused in on the major concepts that they were having trouble with: transpiration pull and phloem pressure, flow. . . . I told them the take-home test was going to be very application-based. We'd have a lot of time to do it, but they had to work on it themselves, with no help from anyone else. I think they really liked it. And when I taught this stuff in class I could teach it in such a way as, "You'd better take notes on this stuff because if you don't you're going to be lost when you go to do your take-home test because you can't copy someone else's notes." Which worked out really well, and it saved class time. It was hard on me because I didn't have that one day of rest with the test— while they're taking the test I can take a deep breath and reassess. (Year Two)

George continued to be fascinated by good student questions. Teaching biology was "much easier a second time around. Now I understand everything a lot better and therefore can be clearer to the students. And can spend more time worrying about whether they're getting it or not, rather than do I understand this."

His typical tests involved the same compromises as the year before. Although he did not use long essay questions on exams, "I do give them sort of mini-essays for homework." George still disliked lecturing and thought that he would like to design a project-based approach so that the content presented was "put out there with a purpose, not just for the sake of having it out there." He was not sanguine about finding a place to teach that way because "anywhere there are going to be students taking the achievement or Regents [tests] or something, there are facts to be mastered."

George still maintained there was no essential content and felt this belief had cost him credibility at his first school.

> Almost every department meeting there we ended up [with] people sort of spouting their knowledge of various subject matters, obliquely, you know. . . . It was just, well should we teach protostomes and dueterostomes? And then we would launch into this debate. Very frustrating. (Year Two)

In his second year George taught both chemistry and biology. When I asked him to compare teaching the two subjects, he presented further thinking about the nature of cause in biology, thinking that parallels his thoughts in student teaching.

> Oh! Well, as I said earlier, I thought it would be very similar, which was a very naive assumption. . . . An answer to a question in chemistry is very different from a satisfying answer to a question in biology. And I think that comes from our experience with questions and answers in our everyday life. We come in with expectations about what a good question is, what a satisfying answer is. And what biology deals with is a lot closer to our everyday experience. . . .
>   In biology, you can go down more layers [than in chemistry] before you run into this sort of conceptual wall where you have to say, because, it just is. . . . Like in genetics, if someone says, "Well, why does that offspring have red eyes?" And I can say, "Because it has one red eye gene and one white eye gene," and they can say, "Well why does that result in red eyes?" And I can say, "Because red is dominant to white." They might stop asking at that point. But if they said, "Why is red dominant to white?" I might be able to talk

biochemically about the enzyme involved in making the red pigment versus not making the red pigment. At that point they might
be satisfied. But they could still ask. . . . Whereas with chemistry,
you're dealing with the most fundamental things in the universe.
And from day one you're running into walls. (Year Two)

George felt that teaching chemistry posed fewer curriculum questions than
did teaching biology because "chemistry, to its credit, is more well-defined."

SUMMARY

George's love of biology and research provided a powerful impetus
for his work at Cornell. From his first interview, it was clear that he worked
to understand the mechanisms and relationships underlying phenomena
and the thinking processes that led to knowledge claims and to new questions in biology. He expressed no doubts about his ability to learn, and his
desire to understand deeply led him to critique the amount of material
presented in Cornell courses. He was critical of the high school curricula
he had to teach because they also covered too much material. I was im-
pressed early on by his critique, his ability to reflect on his Cornell experiences as a junior. However, this critique posed a dilemma he could not
resolve in his teaching.

His view of biology as a complex field, one that could be understood
from several possible perspectives, contributed to his refusal to identify
any particular content as essential. He was most concerned that his students learn to think systematically and rigorously. An important aspect for
this thinking was developing the initial question to be examined. George
never closely examined the role of specific subject matter knowledge in
coming up with testable questions. This emphasis led him to wish to have
a project-based course, one in which material would be applied to some
actual problem. Because of external examinations, though, he doubted he
could ever find a teaching position that would enable him to teach this way.

George recognized that he was a slow learner because he was thinking deeply, making connections and moving beyond memorization. He was
not concerned about his ignorance when he could not answer students'
questions, but was intrigued by the questions.

In his junior year, George had a vision of what students should gain
from a high school biology course, but did not know how to help learners
achieve this goal. His descriptions of his own learning, and his efforts to
gauge student understanding, suggest that he was not fully aware of strategies used to learn and therefore was not explicit about how he could help

his students learn these strategies. For example, he prepared review sheets for students who could not pick out key ideas, but did not talk about helping them to learn how to do this on their own.

When talking about his goals for teaching biology, George's focus was clearly on the science. He loved it when his students were interested and excited about the content, but did not seem to see it as the teacher's responsibility to convince his students that biology was exciting. He wanted his students to leave a lecture or a lab with more questions, but did not consider possible effects on students who were struggling with the content. George's focus on the research aspects of biology, his refusal to identify essential content, and his failure to address some student needs left him with no strong purpose for being a biology teacher, but many reasons for being a biologist.

George was interested in biology for its own sake and for the complex reasoning involved in research and experimentation. He never identified key content as crucial for teaching and in fact resisted efforts to do so. His thinking was complex, and explicit on nearly all the topics we discussed. He said that he enjoyed my research visits, but worried that they constituted an intervention themselves, thus introducing experimenter bias.

Teaching in residential schools created many demands on his time, and he found he had to compromise some of his preferred approaches to teaching and testing because of time constraints. He had criticized the amount of content in Cornell courses because it created conditions that did not allow him to study any area in depth. This frustration continued in all his teaching settings because the need to cover content prevented him from addressing student questions that intrigued him or designing labs that involved inquiry.

The examples of inquiry labs that he provided are somewhat ironic, though, because the results generally were known, such as the effect of exercise on heart rate. However, the known results were based on studies of populations, so that the findings from the sample of students in his classes could have been different.

CHAPTER 8

Some Themes

The new teachers' ideas developed over time, becoming more complex and explicit, but not changing radically. The areas in which these ideas developed varied among the new teachers. Some developed their views about biology; some developed more complex ways to think about students' learning. As teachers, some were able to develop a practice that enabled them to enact their visions of teaching, and others believed that they could never enact their vision of teaching biology. The situations in which the new teachers found themselves when they were employed varied tremendously. All the new teachers found professional help and support, sometimes within their schools and sometimes from other sources. There was no one system of support for these new teachers, and much of the support was serendipitous or the result of active searching by the new teachers. Many of the new teachers faced assignments or arrangements that interfered with their teaching.

WHAT HAVE I LEARNED AS A TEACHER EDUCATOR?

I have shifted my ideas in several ways. In doing this research I have been reminded of my love for biology and my wonder at the complexity of the discipline. The ideas of these new teachers exemplify the richness of the discipline and the difficulties that face those of us wanting to introduce novices to the field. There is no one way to do so because there are so many facets to the discipline.

Subject Matter Knowledge

When I began working in Cornell's teacher education program, I thought that the education course I taught should focus on helping the new teachers understand how their perspectives had been shaped by their knowledge of biology and realize that their students would likely think about biological phenomena quite differently. I did not think that I should concern myself directly with specifics of the new teachers' subject knowledge or learning. Over the course of this study, I have realized that I could have, and should have, helped some of the new teachers to articulate better either their understandings of particular content or their understandings of how they learned that content. Why? Sylvie's story was the one that first sensitized me about this issue. She was not sure about her understanding of specific content in biology, and in the interview I reassured her, focusing on making her feel good about herself. However, the root of her anxiety was her lack of understanding. I would have served her better by going over the material. Also, I might have been able to help her learn study methods that did not depend on sheer memorization.

I have learned from these new teachers that, as a teacher educator, I need a substantial amount of subject matter knowledge. Helping new teachers better understand strategies and methods for learning also would render them better able to help their own students. When I begin to feel overwhelmed by having to know so much, I realize I can help students to learn to monitor and think about their own learning and understandings. I realize that much of the work to examine subject matter can be done without relying on the professor or teacher educator. Pat's story demonstrates how much help peers can provide. So, while my first lesson was that *I*, as teacher educator, must play a more active role to help new teachers understand their biology content, my second realization was that peers, other new teachers, could be even more helpful. Their knowledge, as biology students, will be more up-to-date and relevant, and new teachers will use a range of strategies to learn and can learn about these strategies from each other. As a science teacher educator I certainly should keep abreast of the research in my field, but more important I should work to create a climate that fosters productive exchange among the new teachers.

Delineation of Norms

Fostering a climate that supports sharing of confusions is not easy. George's description of the curriculum deliberations in his first school revealed the posturing and power plays that often underlie discussions of content. Other of the new teachers also spoke of these dynamics, dynamics that rest on norms reinforced in many science classrooms. Like all norms, they primarily are learned subconsciously, internalized, and rarely examined. Barton (1997) analyzed her attempts to construct "a liberatory and inclusive science education." She mused about her goal:

> Even though I would like to think that . . . the students and I will begin to
> create a place in our little classroom for our ideas about science, a shelter from

the ever-present influence of the powerful institution of science and the hierarchical structure of education and society, I know that it is impossible. I know that everything we say and do in our class has been inscribed, at least partially, by the innermost workings of science, education, and society, and all of their associated power arrangements which are emblazoned in our hearts and souls. I know that to shake those power arrangements, to challenge them, is what we must do if we are to construct a liberatory teaching and learning setting, but in order to do this we must be aware of where, how, and why those power arrangements exist. (Barton, 1997, p. 143)

I, too, have aimed to develop a pedagogy that can enable my students to examine and possibly transform their ideas about teaching, learning, and science. I have, with others in the TESM program, tried to nourish in our students the wish to become innovative teachers who will strive to help more of their pupils grasp science and mathematics.

There is evidence in the stories that we in TESM succeeded in imbuing in our new teachers a sense that they would be innovative teachers who would teach in nontraditional ways. We did not do them an unmitigated favor, because they moved into schools that favored traditional teaching. Since beginning this project, and hearing stories from other TESM students in new jobs, I have been more explicit about how much work it requires to change expectations. I have found social constructivist frameworks (e.g., Wertsch, del Rio, & Alvarez, 1995) helpful ways to explain how systems perpetuate themselves. It is not enough to help future teachers examine their own beliefs about teaching and learning. They need also to grasp the meanings maintained in a school, especially when they wish to teach differently. It is often a complex negotiation process to convince students and colleagues of the value of different kinds of assignments. As I have seen successive cohorts of TESM graduates and student teachers deal with the cultures in their schools, I have been far more explicit in pointing out the operation of school culture when working with student teachers, and have tried to point out to them that each school will have its own culture. In trying to make the operation of culture more obvious, I have moved to make my own teaching decisions more clear to students to help them understand the factors shaping my thinking. And I have used their reactions to some of the things I expect them to do to examine their assumptions about school culture.

A Personal Vision

I have learned how crucial it is that I, as teacher educator, help each prospective teacher develop an elaborated personal vision of what he or she wishes to accomplish as a teacher, a vision that includes subject matter and the development of students, as learners and as humans. I believe that this is the kind of reflection that is most important. LaBoskey (1994) pointed out that reflection is a term much less often defined than used. When I began this study, I was most concerned with helping new teachers gather evidence to use in determining whether they had reached their goals, whether their pupils had developed the hoped-for understandings or skills. Gathering evidence from a range of sources is not an easy task, nor is it unimportant. Since doing this study, though, I hope also to help new teachers think seriously about their goals. This is a kind of reflection that should last for a career as the base for continuing development.

ISSUES RELATED TO POLICY AND REFORM

Induction

When hired, all the new teachers received support of some kind. Much of the support served to constrain innovation. New teachers were helped to become like those teachers already in the school, and it appeared that few of these teachers considered themselves as innovators. The new teachers were not inducted into a general profession of teaching, but into the system of the school where they taught. Help from more experienced colleagues was in the form of shared materials—exams, lab exercises, schedules—and served to shape the new teacher into the kind of teacher expected in that school. This localism parallels the individualism of teachers; just as teachers often practice in isolation from each other, schools develop as systems in isolation from outside influences.

Constraints

It would be a mistake to blame individual schools for being conservative because there were many outside forces shaping what could be done. External examinations, whether statewide Regents tests in New York or achievement tests taken for college entrance, set the curriculum for the high school teachers. The curriculum was full of material, which meant that time-consuming activities designed to foster more in-depth understanding had to be curtailed, if not jettisoned.

External examinations and school expectations also limited the kinds of examinations the new teachers gave, because new teachers had to prepare their pupils to be successful on multiple choice examinations. When new teachers had to limit the kinds of assessments they used, they learned less about their students and thus had less information on which to base changes.

The students of the new teachers attempted to negotiate academic tasks and shape the new teachers' actions to fit their own expectations (e.g., Britzman, 1986). Several of the new teachers did more lecturing than they wished because their students were used to taking notes and resisted preparing for discussions.

Some of the constraints might have been possible to control at the local level. Although they could easily seem trivial, some factors had a strong impact on the new teachers' opportunities. Having no classroom of one's own, in which to set up equipment or supplies, is a real problem for biology teachers. Trying to run a complex laboratory activity in only one period posed problems. Being assigned classes with students who were hard to work with for a beginning teacher added to the stress of the first year.

Will the Real Reform Please Stand Up?

The rhetoric in the national reform documents is quite wonderful. These documents present new visions and strong arguments supporting the changes they advocate. There is evidence of the benefits that could accrue if the reforms were adopted. But in my talks with the new teachers, I saw little evidence that these reform suggestions were being offered to teachers in a coherent fashion. In fact, some of the workshops they told me about presented visions of teaching in contrast to the national reform efforts. It seemed that the new teachers were exhorted to try a range of things in order to be up-to-date, with little attempt to evaluate the quality of the approaches. Sylvie described the effects that she observed on a teacher who struggled to be in the vanguard. There are so many vanguards that one can drive oneself into exhaustion trying to keep up. It is difficult for teachers to decide what to do. Given the plethora of calls to teach differently, it is also easy to sympathize with more experienced teachers who have become inured to calls to change.

WHAT IS IT LIKE TO BE A NEW TEACHER?

Obviously, these stories all show that it is not easy to be a new teacher. During one of our informal chats Sylvie told me she thought my research was valuable because it would help other new teachers. Becoming a teacher generally seemed a harder process for the women. The four women were less confident about themselves as learners. They worried about their subject matter knowledge, their ability to answer questions and to explain their judgments to students, and they worried about how they would be perceived by their students. The new teachers had to familiarize themselves with their curricula, to develop a sense of the narrative that a good course should create and form the bases for their pedagogical content knowledge (Shulman, 1986). It took time to learn what their students would do and how they needed to be encouraged and what skills they needed to develop. The new teachers were all surprised by some of the difficulties their students had, not necessarily with the content but with organizing their learning. There are many things with which a teacher can be concerned.

Being an innovative teacher is not something that happens as a result of graduating from a teacher education program. Becoming a teacher takes time. Finding good materials that support new teaching practices takes more time. Learning to modify or develop materials takes even more time. On occasion the new teachers seemed to apologize to me for using lessons they had borrowed from others or lessons they did not think were very creative. I believe I, and perhaps other faculty in TESM, had created the sense that to be innovative one had to develop all materials *de novo*.

The new teachers found it imperative to find ways to delimit their work so that it did not demand too much time and energy. Several of the new teachers tried different formats for quizzes and tests, but frequently found that grading the large number of these tests consistently was exhausting and time-consuming.

And the new teachers had to come to accept that their profession is an uncertain one, one full of surprises that are not consistently pleasant. McDonald (1992) wrote about the uncertainty of teaching. In his view, reform initiatives generally have failed because they have refused to acknowledge the fundamental uncertainty of teaching, uncertainty that will not yield to reformulated procedures, rules, goals, or outcome measures. McDonald (1992) saw the acceptance of uncertainty as central to professional growth.

> I dare to offer a different message only because I trust that when one opens oneself to the real complexities and uncertainties of life—even in precious realms—one gains not only a better understanding of life but also more grace and inventiveness in living. . . . I believe that an acknowledgement of fundamental uncertainty can enhance practical confidence and directness, foster productivity, and even raise hopes. (p. 7)

The enormity of the act of embracing uncertainty is illustrated in the stories of these new teachers, particularly when they practiced in settings that attempted to render teaching an entirely rational and standardized process.

Just as I had to deal with the uncertainty of doing longitudinal research that evolved over many years, the new teachers have dealt with the uncertainty of trying to understand their complex and constantly changing classrooms.

References

American Association for the Advancement of Science. (1993). *Benchmarks for science literacy*. Oxford: Oxford University Press.

Barton, A. C. (1997). Liberatory science education: Weaving connections between feminist theory and science education. *Curriculum Inquiry, 27*(2), 141–163.

Berlak, A., & Berlak, H. (1981). *Dilemmas of schooling*. New York: Methuen.

Biological Sciences Curriculum Studies. (1970). *Biology teachers' handbook* (3rd ed.). New York: Wiley.

Britzman, D. P. (1986). Cultural myths in the making of a teacher: Biography and social structure in teacher education. *Harvard Educational Review, 56*(4), 442–456.

Brown, L. M., & Gilligan, C. (1992). *Meeting at the crossroads*. Cambridge, MA: Harvard University Press.

Buchmann, M. (1992). Dilemmas and virtues in research communication. *Curriculum Inquiry, 22*(3), 313–329.

Calderhead, J. (Ed.). (1987). *Exploring teachers' thinking*. London: Cassell.

Clandinin, D. J., Davies, A., Hogan, P., & Kennard, B. (Eds.). (1993). *Learning to teach, teaching to learn: Stories of collaboration in teacher education*. New York: Teachers College Press.

Clark, C. M., & Peterson, P. L. (1986). Teachers' thought processes. In M. C. Wittrock (Ed.), *Handbook of research on teaching* (3rd ed.; pp. 255–296). New York: Macmillan.

Cobb, P. (1994). Where is the mind? Constructivist and sociocultural perspectives on mathematical development. *Educational Researcher, 23*(7), 13–20.

Connelly, E. M., & Clandinin, D. J. (1986). On narrative method, biography and narrative unities in the study of teaching. (ERIC Document Reproduction Service No. ED 277 664)

Connelly, E. M., & Clandinin, D. J. (1990). Stories of experience and narrative inquiry. *Educational Researcher, 19*(4), 2–14.

Cummins, C. L. (1995). The nature of science as communicated by science fairs: Is experimentation really the only scientific method? In F. Finley, D. Allchin, D. Rhees, & S. Fifield (Eds.), *Proceedings of the Third International History, Philosophy, and Science Teaching Conference* (Vol. I, pp. 277–287). Minneapolis: University of Minnesota.

Cummins, C. L., & Remsen, J. V. (1992). The importance of distinguishing ultimate from proximate causation in the teaching and learning of biology. In S. Hills (Ed.), *Proceedings of the Second International Conference for History and Philosophy of Science in Science Teaching* (Vol. I, pp. 201–210). Kingston, Ontario:

Mathematics, Science, Technology and Teacher Education Group and Faculty of Education, Queen's University.

Davis, B., & Sumara, D. J. (1997). Cognition, complexity, and teacher education. *Harvard Educational Review, 76*(1), 105–125.

DeBoer, G. E. (1991). *A history of ideas in science education*. New York: Teachers College Press.

Driver, R., Asoko, H., Leach, J., Mortimer, E., & Scott, P. (1994). Constructing scientific knowledge in the classroom. *Educational Researcher, 23*(7), 5–12.

Driver, R., Guesne, E., & Tiberghien, A. (Eds.). (1985). *Children's ideas in science*. Philadelphia: Open University Press.

Erickson, F. (1986). Qualitative methods in research on teaching. In M. C. Wittrock (Ed.), *Handbook of research on teaching* (3rd ed.; pp. 119–161). New York: Macmillan.

Feiman-Nemser, S., & Featherstone, H. (Eds.). (1992). *Exploring teaching: Reinventing an introductory course*. New York: Teachers College Press.

Gilbert, J. K., Osborne, R. J., & Fensham, P. J. (1982). Children's science and its consequences for teaching. *Science Education, 66*(4), 623–633.

Grimmett, P. P., & Erickson, G. L. (Eds.). (1988). *Reflection in teacher education*. New York: Teachers College Press.

Gudmundsdottir, S. (1996). The teller, the tale and the one being told: The narrative nature of the research interview. *Curriculum Inquiry, 26*(3), 293–306.

Gunstone, R. F., White, R. T., & Fensham, P. (1988). Developments in style and purpose of research on the learning of science. *Journal of Research in Science Teaching, 25*(7), 513–529.

Helm, H., & Novak, J. D. (1983). *Proceedings of the International Seminar on Misconceptions in Science and Mathematics*. Ithaca, NY: Cornell University.

Hodson, D. (1996). Practical work in school science: Exploring some directions for change. *International Journal of Science Education, 18*(7), 755–760.

Kelly, G. A. (1955). *The psychology of personal constructs* (Vol. 1). New York: Norton.

Kuhn, T. (1970). *The structure of scientific revolutions*. Chicago: University of Chicago Press.

LaBoskey, V. K. (1994). *Development of reflective practice: A study of preservice teachers*. New York: Teachers College Press.

Louden, W. (1995). "Just one story": Reading and writing about teaching. *Curriculum Inquiry, 25*(1), 111–113.

Loughran, J. (1994). Bridging the gap: An analysis of the needs of second-year science teachers. *Science Education, 78*(4), 365–386.

Mayr, E. (1982). *The growth of biological thought: Diversity, evolution, and inheritance*. Cambridge, MA: Belknap Press of Harvard University Press.

Mayr, E. (1988). *Toward a new philosophy of biology: Observations of an evolutionist*. Cambridge, MA: Belknap Press of Harvard University Press.

McDiarmid, G. W. (1990). Challenging prospective teachers' beliefs during early field experience. *Journal of Teacher Education, 41*(3), 12–20.

McDonald, J. P. (1992). *Teaching: Making sense of an uncertain craft*. New York: Teachers College Press.

McNiff, J. (1993). *Teaching as learning: An action research approach*. London & New York: Routledge.

Mishler, E. G. (1986). *Research interviewing: Context and narrative.* Newbury Park, CA: Sage.

National Research Council. (1996). *National Science Education Standards.* Washington, DC: National Academy Press.

National Science Teachers Association. (1992). *Scope, sequence, and coordination of secondary science* (Vol. 1). Washington, DC: Author.

Nespor, J. (1987). The role of beliefs in the practice of teaching. *Journal of Curriculum Studies, 4,* 317–328.

Nespor, J., & Barylske, J. (1991). Narrative discourse and teacher knowledge. *American Educational Research Journal, 28*(4), 805–823.

Novak, J. D., & Gowin, D. B. (1984). *Learning how to learn.* London: Cambridge University Press.

Peshkin, A. (1985). Virtuous subjectivity: In the participant-observer's I's. In D. Berk & K. Smith (Eds.), *Exploring clinical methods for social research* (pp. 239–252). Newbury Park, CA: Sage.

Peshkin, A. (1988). In search of subjectivity—one's own. *Educational Researcher, 17*(7), 17–22.

Polkinghorne, D. E. (1988). *Narrative knowing and the human sciences.* Albany: State University of New York Press.

Posner, G. J., Strike, K. A., Hewson, P. W., & Gertzog, W. A. (1982). Accommodation of a scientific conception: Toward a theory of conceptual change. *Science Education, 66,* 211–217.

Schön, D. A. (1983). *The reflective practitioner: How professionals think in action.* New York: Basic Books.

Shulman, L. S. (1986). Those who understand: Knowledge growth in teaching. *Educational Researcher, 15*(2), 4–14.

Stoddart, T. (1991, April). *Reconstructing teaching candidates' views of teaching and learning.* Paper presented at the annual meeting of the American Educational Research Association, Chicago.

Stofflett, R. T. (1994). The accommodation of science pedagogical knowledge: The application of conceptual change constructs to teacher education. *Journal of Research in Science Teaching, 31*(8), 787–810.

Stofflett, R. T., & Stoddart, T. (1994). The ability to understand and use conceptual change pedagogy as a function of prior content learning experience. *Journal of Research in Science Teaching, 31*(1), 31–51.

Strike, K. A., & Posner, G. J. (1992). A revisionist theory of conceptual change. In R. A. Duschl & R. J. Hamilton (Eds.), *Philosophy of science, cognitive psychology, and educational theory and practice* (pp. 147–176). Albany: State University of New York Press.

Taylor, C. (1982). Interpretation and the sciences of man. In E. Bredo & W. Feinberg (Eds.), *Knowledge and values in social and educational research* (pp. 153–186). Philadelphia: Temple University Press.

Trumbull, D. J. (1987). Practitioner knowledge: An examination of the artistry in teaching. *The Journal of Educational Thought, 20,* 113–124.

Trumbull, D. J. (1990). Evolving images of teaching: Reflections of one teacher. *Curriculum Inquiry, 20*(2), 161–182.

Trumbull, D. J. (1991). Education 301. *Teaching Education, 3*(2), 145–150.

Trumbull, D. J. (1996). There's nothing that bugs people more than sort of remembering: Ambiguity in the growth of a science teacher. *Curriculum Inquiry, 26*(1), 47–70.

Trumbull, D. J., & Slack, M. J. (1991). Learning to ask, listen, and analyze. *International Journal of Science Education, 13*(2), 129–142.

Van Manen, M. (1990). *Researching lived experience.* Albany: State University of New York Press.

Wertsch, J. V., del Rio, P., & Alvarez, A. (1995). *Sociocultural studies of mind.* Cambridge, UK: Cambridge University Press.

West, L. H. T., & Pines, A. L. (Eds.). (1985). *Cognitive structure and conceptual change.* Orlando: Academic Press.

White, R. T. (1996). The link between the laboratory and learning. *International Journal of Science Education, 18*(7), 761–774.

Woolnough, B. E. (1991). Setting the scene. In B. E. Woolnough (Ed.), *Practical science.* Bristol, PA: Open University Press.

Index

About the Author

Deborah J. Trumbull taught biology in several community colleges before completing a Ph.D. in educational psychology at the University of Illinois Urbana-Champaign. She has taught a core education class for Cornell's preservice teachers and has supervised student teachers in many successive cohorts. She has published articles in *Curriculum Inquiry, Science Education, International Journal of Science Education, Journal of Educational Thought, Journal of Curriculum Studies,* and *Journal of Curriculum and Supervision.* In addition to continuing to study how people become teachers, her most recent research effort examines how teachers help their students conduct science inquiries using observations of birds at feeders and data collected by classrooms across North America.